Forensic Document Examination for Legal Professionals: A Science-Based Approach

MICHAEL N. WAKSHULL

Forensic Document Examination for Legal Professionals: A Scientific Approach
Copyright © 2019 Michael N. Wakshull

All rights reserved. No part of this book may be reproduced by any means without the written permission of the author, except for short passages used in crticial reviews.

ISBN: 978-0-9857294-5-5
Library of Congress Control Number: 2018931818

Table of Contents

Figures ix

Introduction 1
Who will benefit by reading this book? 2
Document examiners can be disqualified or their testimony excluded 2
Your examiner must have the proper qualifications 3
Common pitfalls of document examination 4
Why is it difficult to select a qualified document examiner? 6
Don't lose your case by failing to prepare 7
Document examination is complex 8
Document examiners follow a code of ethics 8
What to expect from your document examiner 11

Essential aspects of forensic document examination 13
What type of documents are examined? 14
Terminology used by document examiners 16
Written documents 17
The need for a science-based approach 18

Authentication of documents 21
Federal Rules of Evidence §1001 offers several important
definitions. 23

Laws for document examination 23
California Evidence Code. 25
Texas Rules of Evidence 26
   Rule 1001: Definitions 26
Louisiana Code of Evidence 26
   Article 1001:Definitions 26
The law of expert testimony 27
   Frye v. United States 27
   Daubert v. Merrell Dow Pharmaceuticals 27
   Additional Supreme Court cases. 28
   Does Frye apply to forensic document examiners?. 29

Standards for forensic document examiners 30
The SAFE Standards 32
The SWGDOC Standards 32
Huber & Hedrick proposed 21 elements for discrimination of
handwriting.. 33
Document examiners' opinions 34

Document examiners' tools 39

Each assignment is a project. 46
Mathematics and probability theory in document examination 48

Examination of handwriting 50
Exemplars versus questioned documents 50
   Examination Procedure. 51
Collection of exemplars 53
   Compare similar forms of handwriting. 53

Types of exemplars................................... 54
   Existing writing exemplars 55
   Potential problems with photocopy exemplars 56
   Know the provenance of your data 57
   Request exemplars.................................. 58

Variability of handwriting 64
No two people write alike............................. 64
No person writes exactly the same twice.................. 67
Types of variation.................................... 71
   Common cause variation.............................. 71
   Special cause variation 71
Use of statistical techniques 72
   Measure angles of the writing.......................... 75

Authentication of handwriting........................ 78
Simulation of writing................................. 79
Writing direction as a differentiator 82
Disguised writing..................................... 83
Infirmity.. 85
Verification of exemplars – refer to standard............... 86
Robosigning... 89
Compare signatures using Photoshop.................... 90

Altered documents 92
Using infrared light to discover ink alterations 92
Cut and paste alterations 95
   Manual cut and paste alterations....................... 97
   Discover a cut and paste when a source document is missing .. 100
   Alterations using different printers 102
Determine line sequence for potential handwritten alteration. 102
Examining torn documents 109
Ink dating 111

Paper dating 112
Photocopiers and laser printers used for alterations. 113
   Trash marks *113*
   Inaccurate reproduction of a document by a photocopy machine 114
   Machine identification code technology in color laser printers. . *115*
   Photocopied versus original signatures. *115*
   Color photocopiers. *117*

The future of document examination. **119**
Signatures on digital tablets 120
Electronic signatures on real estate documents 123
Examination of electronic documents. 124
   PDF files *125*
   Email. *127*
   Scanned files and photographs *129*

Standard operating procedures **132**
Example of a portion of a standard operating procedure. 133
Summary 136

Are document examiners better than laypeople at identifying handwriting? **138**
Discussion 138
Challenges to the validity of document examination 141
Results from the National Academy of Sciences 143
Federal Rules of Evidence Rule 702 145

Document examiners must meet legal standards **145**
Frye v. United States. 146
Daubert v. Merrill-Dow Pharmaceuticals 147
   Applying the scientific method *148*
Issues with the error rate requirement. 150

Summary for error rate *154*

Can forensic experts overcome their biases? **156**
What is bias? 156
Laboratory bias. 159
Bias is ever-present 160
Contextual bias 161
   Knowing the context encourages bias *161*
   Bias begins at the outset. *162*
   How to reduce bias *162*
   Framing the problem *163*
   Confirmation bias. *164*
The scientific method 166

Document examiner's reports. **167**
Rule 26 Report. 168

Selecting a document examiner **171**
Follow a generally accepted practice 172
Perform accurate assessments 172
Ask the examiner to describe the methodology to be used for the case 172
   Establishing handwriting variability *173*
   A case of written initials *174*
Code of ethics 175
Certificates and education 177
Investigate your prospective document examiner 179
Internet search methodology 179
Is your first question the correct question? 183
Services and deliverables you should expect from your document examiner 184

Final thoughts..................................189

References....................................192

Index...195

About the Author..............................206

Figures

Figure 1.1 Did one of the two people write the document? 15
Figure 1.2 How a hypothesis is accepted..................................19
Figure 3.1 SWGDOC Document Examiner's Opinions............35
Figure 3.2 SAFE Document Examiner's Opinions....................35
Figure 4.1 Digital microscope..39
Figure 4.2 Optical microscope...40
Figure 4.3 Viewing scope...40
Figure 4.4 Loupe...41
Figure 4.5 Ruler..41
Figure 4.6 Photoshop..42
Figure 4.7 Computer...42
Figure 4.8 Flatbed scanner...42
Figure 4.9 ESDA...43
Figure 4.10 VSC..43
Figure 4.11 HSI Examiner...44
Figure 4.12 Digital camera..44
Figure 4.13 Calipers...45
Figure 6.1 Example of problem with photocopies....................61

Figure 7.1 Writing of two people 64
Figure 7.2 Writing Zones 66
Figure 7.3 Inter-Writer Variability 67
Figure 7.4 Intra-Writer Variability 68
Figure 7.5 Writing habits 70
Figure 7.6 Control chart of the natural variation of ratios 73
Figure 7.7 Natural Variation of the Angle of Writing 76
Figure 8.1 Freehand Simulation 79
Figure 8.2 Simulation 80
Figure 8.3 Simulation 81
Figure 8.4 Writing direction 82
Figure 8.5 NEGA software for writing direction 83
Figure 8.6 Disguised writing 83
Figure 8.7 Infirm person's writing 85
Figure 8.8 Infirm and Drug Side Effects 86
Figure 8.9 Variation of valid signatures 87
Figure 8.10 Hindi Writing 88
Figure 8.11 Robosigning 89
Figure 8.12 Rubber stamp 90
Figure 8.13 Signature comparison match 90
Figure 8.14 Compare two questioned signatures 91
Figure 9.1 Electromagnetic Spectrum 92
Figure 9.2 Infrared light 93
Figure 9.3 Image in white light 94
Figure 9.4 Image in infrared light 95
Figure 9.5 Altered document 95
Figure 9.6 Cut and paste 98
Figure 9.7 Cut and paste overlay 99
Figure 9.8 Cut and paste evidence 99
Figure 9.9 Cut and paste without a source file 100
Figure 9.10 Difference in printers 102
Figure 9.11 Line sequence illusion 103

Figure 9.12 Line sequence 104
Figure 9.13 Line sequence infrared 105
Figure 9.14 Infrared luminescence..106
Figure 9.15 Blue ballpoint ink over toner 107
Figure 9.16 Black ballpoint ink over toner................................107
Figure 9.17 The image in Figure 9.16 viewed with NEGA software..108
Figure 9.18 Which line came first, white light 108
Figure 9.19 Examination of writing with NEGA software 109
Figure 9.20 Photocopy of an allegedly torn page 110
Figure 9.21 Watermark with a date indicator...........................112
Figure 9.22 Trash Marks...113
Figure 9.23 Photocopy problems..114
Figure 9.24 Ink Versus Toner..116
Figure 9.25 Writing without magnification 117
Figure 9.26 Writing with magnification...................................117
Figure 9.27 Close-up image of a color photocopy....................118
Figure 10.1 Signature on a digital tablet 120
Figure 10.2 Data Points..121
Figure 10.3 Plot of electronically captured writing 122
Figure 10.4 Plot of writing showing data points 122
Figure 10.5 Evidence of an electronic signature placed using SignNow 124
Figure 10.6 Example of Preflight tool in Adobe Acrobat Pro ...126
Figure 10.7 Example of Adobe Acrobat metadata properties....127
Figure 10.8 Example of email headers in Microsoft Outlook...128
Figure 10.9 Photograph of a damaged lottery ticket 129
Figure 10.10 Metadata for the image in Figure 10.9 130
Figure 12.1 Black box process...141

Introduction

The courts currently require more rigorous, science-based, verifiable evidence to support the opinion offered by all testifying expert witnesses.

The publication *Strengthening Forensic Science in the United States* by the National Academy of Sciences (NAS) reported that there is too much bias in forensic disciplines, including handwriting examination. The NAS-reported that opinions are based too much on subjective analysis rather than objective, science-based analysis.

Both the Kelly-Frye and Daubert rulings require use of a scientific approach for developing and presenting opinions of expert witnesses.

Forensic document examination is the fascinating scientific discipline used to determine the authenticity of documents. It includes the analysis of handwriting, inks, photocopies, printed documents, computer-generated documents, and any other form of document. I had a case where the document in question was handwritten on piece of toilet paper. Another was written on the side of a portable outhouse.

Later in this chapter you will find definitions of the words authenticate and authentication. These definitions come from legal dictionary and evidence code from different jurisdictions. When document examiners opine that a document or aspect of the document such as handwriting is authentic, they are saying the subject matter is that which purports to be.

You'll notice in this book that the term "expert" is intentionally omitted from the description of the document examiner. Only a court can designate a person as an expert.

The discipline is largely misunderstood by the public, by victims of forgery and document alteration, and most importantly by legal professionals, court employees on all levels, and jurors.

This misunderstanding leads to failed attempts to correctly determine the guilt or innocence of the alleged creator of the document in question.

WHO WILL BENEFIT BY READING THIS BOOK?

This in-depth guide is a detailed review of forensic document examination designed to enable attorneys and other legal professionals to prepare successfully for criminal and civil trials requiring the authentication of documents.

The keyword here is, successfully.

This book covers many little-known aspects document examination. Reading this book will help you become aware of potential pitfalls in your case. It will help you navigate the aspects of document authentication to make success at trial more likely when the case turns on the authenticity of a document in question.

DOCUMENT EXAMINERS CAN BE DISQUALIFIED OR THEIR TESTIMONY EXCLUDED

In the case 1:10-CR-110, United Sates of America v. Mary Revels, in the United States District Court Eastern District of Tennessee at Chattanooga, an examiner was disqualified for the inability to demonstrate sufficient education and training. The United States District Court of Eastern Tennessee excluded the defendant's document examiner's testimony. The Court ruled he was not qualified to offer expert testimony.

In the ruling the court wrote,

> "On the surface, Mr. [Examiner's] credentials are noteworthy, and they certainly impressed Defendant enough to retain him as an opinion witness. Yet, in this field, due diligence necessitates probing beneath the surface, and in Mr. [Examiner's] case, even a small amount of probing would have unearthed a rather different picture."

The defendant was not granted leave to retain a new document examiner.

In the case of Almeciga v. Center For Investigative Reporting, Inc., et al., case No. 15-cv-4319 (JSR) in the United States District Court, Southern District of New York the plaintiff's document examiner was disqualified. The Court ruled,

> "In particular, the Court grants defendant's motion to exclude [plaintiff's document examiner's] "expert" testimony, finding that handwriting analysis in general is unlikely to meet the admissibility requirements of Federal Rule of Evidence 702 and that, in any event, [plaintiff's document examiner's] testimony does not meet those standards."

The document examiner's names have been omitted from the text of this book.

Your examiner must have the proper qualifications

Selecting the best forensic examiner for your case can mean the difference between winning and losing. Just as the practice of law is specialized, the discipline of forensic document examination covers many areas of practice. You need to find the document examiner who specializes in the type of case you are pursuing.

For example, a handwriting examiner may not be the best person to examine a document typed on a typewriter or printed using a computer printer. You may require the services of the person who specializes in the examination of typewritten documents or a print process examiner. Conversely, a skilled print process examiner may not be experienced in handwriting examination.

The last thing you want to happen is for your document examiner to state in deposition or trial testimony they do not have proper training or knowledge in the skills for performing the case at hand. An honest document examiner will refer the case outside of their skillset to an examiner who specializes in the necessary skills.

Admissibility of your forensic examiner's testimony can enhance or ruin your case before the court. This book clarifies the court requirements for an expert witness to testify at trial or formal hearing.

COMMON PITFALLS OF DOCUMENT EXAMINATION

The concepts explained within will to help you avoid the common pitfalls that occur when using the science of forensic document examination. This book:

- Illustrates the types of cases document examiners investigate.
- Offers detailed insight into the work of forensic document examiners.
- Dispels misunderstandings surrounding
    - The work a forensic document examiner performs.
    - The methods used by a document examiner.
    - The opinions reached.
- Explains how to vet a document examiner prior to retention to work on a case.

- Presents the best ways attorneys can partner with a document examiner to learn the strength of their case and develop the theme.
- Identifies deliverables you should require from your document examiner.

The ability of a forensic examiner to speak to a lay audience is necessary for testimony in trial, deposition, or alternative dispute resolution (ADR) hearings. A pitfall is retaining a forensic examiner who does not understand how to present their opinions to people who are not educated in their discipline.

Your examiner must be able to convey the theories and methods used to arrive at the stated opinions. These ideas must be conveyed in a manner that teaches the listeners, be they the opposing attorneys, judge, or jury.

Another pitfall may be that the document examiner does not own the equipment necessary to perform the investigative work. In deposition during a recent case, the opposing examiner was asked why he did not use the necessary equipment to differentiate inks on handwritten documents. He admitted he did not own equipment to perform this analysis. Yet he had accepted the case for which he was not qualified to perform the work.

There are times when document examiners rely on templates for writing their reports. The document examiner may state that certain equipment or procedures were used for the examination. Although these equipment and procedures are embedded within the template, they may not be applicable to the examination at hand.

Ask the document examiner whether they use templates for their reports. If they state that certain equipment was used, ask them how they used it. An opposing document examiner will discover this inconsistency when reading the report.

WHY IS IT DIFFICULT TO SELECT A QUALIFIED DOCUMENT EXAMINER?

The first problem is, the discipline has neither licensing requirements nor standard training. Although there is a standard that describes guidance for minimum education and training for a forensic document examiner, there is no common approach to implementing this guidance.

Generally accepted practices are set by industry standards, yet the skills and education demonstrated by document examiners varies greatly. Many industry standards are described in chapter 2.

As an attorney or hiring agent, it is important for you to hire the best forensic examiner possible. You want someone who will provide an honest opinion about whether the evidence supports the claims of your client.

In the above-mentioned case in which the forensic document examiner was disqualified, one reason was that he had not been properly trained and educated. The person under whom he studied had been disqualified by a court as not being qualified to testify as a document examiner.

Upon simple investigation using Google, Bing, Yahoo, and other Internet search techniques, you can easily discover aspects of a document examiner's past that offer a reason to question their credibility. As an attorney, you can use tools such as Lexus-Nexus and Trialsmith to learn about your document examiner's performance in other cases.

Chapter 10 presents legal cases that define whether a document examiner is qualified to perform the scope of work and whether they are qualified to testify as an expert witness.

This will help you, as a legal professional who will partner with a forensic document examiner, to discover the questions to ask your prospective forensic partner to determine whether they are qualified and equipped to work on your case.

When the evidence supports the attorney's theory of the case, the attorney and document examiner work together to develop the strategy for presenting the case at deposition, alternative dispute resolution hearing, and/or trial. This book will help the attorney work with the document examiner to develop effective strategies.

Don't lose your case by failing to prepare

You need a document examiner who thinks and acts like a detective. The document examiner should begin by looking at the big picture regarding the document. The big picture may include the overall structure of the writing, type of writing, placement of the writing on the page or relative to lines on the page, type of paper and other major aspects of the writing or the document. The examiner will then delve into the details of the writing or questioned alteration to learn the truth about the case.

These details provide the core of your presentation as it applies to document examination.

Recently a client called me. He said he had been surprised at trial when the opposing side presented evidence by a forensic document examiner who had showed with certainty that his client had not written the handwritten text on a document.

I asked him to scan and send the document and supporting evidence for review. If I found different results, he wanted me to appear the next day to refute the claim by the opposing document examiner.

After completing the examination, I found that two reasons the evidence was insufficient to determine whether his client did or did not execute the handwriting. First, there were an insufficient number of exemplars. Second, the variability among the exemplars made determining the common attributes of the person's writing difficult.

He presented my statement and CV to the opposing counsel. The opposing document examiner's opinion suddenly changed to "inconclusive" on whether the person had written the document. The handwriting was no longer at issue.

DOCUMENT EXAMINATION IS COMPLEX

Many famous cases in the last century have turned on the results of handwriting identification, including the Lindberg baby kidnapping, the Mormon Will, the Salamander Letter, the Howard Hughes diary scandal, the Hitler diaries, and many others.

Handwriting has been examined in unsuccessful attempts to solve the JonBenét Ramsey murder and many other cases. In many cases, document examiners' analyses resulted in divergent opinions about whether a particular person wrote the document.

Cases such as Clifford Irving's Howard Hughes autobiography and Mark Hofmann's Salamander letter have fooled experienced document examiners who opined the documents were authentic when they were shown to be forgeries.

Therefore, you need a document examiner who thinks and works like a detective.

DOCUMENT EXAMINERS FOLLOW A CODE OF ETHICS

Document examiners are hired investigators. They advocate for neither side in a dispute. Their ethical allegiance is to the evidence rather than either side in a legal dispute. As an attorney, your objective is to learn the truth of the evidence.

Ask your prospective document examiner whether they are a member of a non-profit association.

Examiners who are members of professional organizations such as the National Association of Document Examiners (NADE), American Society of Questioned Document Examiners (ASQDE), or Scientific Association of Forensic Examiners (SAFE), subscribe to a code of ethics which prohibits improperly supporting the desired outcome of any party, including the party who hired the document examiner.

In September, 2016, the United States Department of Justice and National Institute of Standards and Technology (NIST) issued a *National Code of Ethics and Professional Responsibility for the Forensic Sciences*. A recommendation was made that all forensic science service providers and certifying bodies in the forensic sciences adopt the code of ethics.

1. Accurately represent his/her education, training, experience, and areas of expertise.
2. Pursue professional competency through training, proficiency testing, certification, and presentation and publication of research findings.
3. Commit to continuous learning in the forensic disciplines and stay abreast of new findings, equipment and techniques.
4. Promote validation and incorporation of new technologies, guarding against the use of non-valid methods in casework and the misapplication of validated methods.
5. Avoid tampering, adulteration, loss, or unnecessary consumption of evidentiary materials.
6. Avoid participation in any case where there are personal, financial, employment-related or other conflicts of interest. Conduct full, fair and unbiased examinations, leading to independent, impartial, and objective opinions and conclusions.
7. Make and retain full, contemporaneous, clear and accurate written records of all examinations and tests conducted and conclusions drawn, in sufficient detail to allow meaningful review and assessment by an independent person competent in the field.
8. Base conclusions on generally-accepted procedures supported by sufficient data, standards and controls, not on political pressure or other outside influence.
9. Do not render conclusions that are outside one's expertise.

10. Prepare reports in unambiguous terms, clearly distinguishing data from interpretations and opinions, and disclosing all known associated limitations that prevent invalid inferences or mislead the judge or jury.
11. Do not alter reports or other records, or withhold information from reports for strategic or tactical litigation advantage.
12. Present accurate and complete data in reports, oral and written presentations and testimony based on good scientific practices and validated methods.
13. Communicate honestly and fully, once a report is issued, with all parties (investigators, prosecutors, defense attorneys, and other expert witnesses), unless prohibited by law.
14. Document and notify management or quality assurance personnel of adverse events, such as an unintended mistake or a breach of ethical, legal, scientific standards, or questionable conduct.
15. Ensure reporting, through proper management channels, to all impacted scientific and legal parties of any adverse event that affects a previously issued report or testimony.

Document examiners, regardless of their association with professional organizations, still need to be vetted to ensure they have the proper skills to work on your case. Ask whether they have worked on a similar case and how they will approach the work on your case.

At times, attorneys as well as laypeople will report to a document examiner that a case is straightforward. However, the trained document examiner may determine that a case is more complex than it appears to the untrained eye.

This book explains the intricacies a document examiner may experience when reaching an opinion. This will help the layperson see the complexity of the profession so they can appreciate the value of the examiner's contribution.

What to expect from your document examiner

Document examiners express their results as opinions rather than conclusions or fact. Document examiners do not prove a statement. They use evidence presented to investigate a case. Based on the evidence at hand they offer an opinion on the story told by the evidence.

Generally, extraneous information such as witness' statements, where a document was discovered, etc. do not play into their opinion when handwriting is at issue.

When authentication of a physical document is at issue, location of discovery and other contextual information may be needed.

Reporting opinions contrary to the retaining party's expected outcome is valuable. It aids the attorney by showing that the client may not have a valid case.

I have had numerous cases where the retaining attorney realized there was no reason to proceed with the case because the results did not support their client's contention. The attorney always told me they wanted to know the truth as they did not want to proceed with a non-meritorious case.

In one instance, an attorney wanted to retain my services for a case where his client stated he did not sign a contract. Exemplar documents were not forthcoming. The attorney's client later admitted in a deposition to having signed the document. We did not go forward with the case.

In another case, the attorney sought authorization from his clients to retain my services. His clients alleged they had not signed a contract. When he asked permission to retain my services, the clients remembered they probably signed the contract.

In a recent case, the attorney's client claimed she had a holographic will written by her aunt which left the entire estate to the niece. Examination showed the will was written by the attorney's client, the niece to whom the estate was willed.

These examples demonstrate the benefit of engaging a forensic document examiner as part of the pre-litigation investigation of the merits of the case. Black's Law Dictionary Tenth Edition (Garner, 2014) defines *forensic* as, "Used in suitable courts of law or public debate."

Chapter 1

Essential aspects of forensic document examination

Forensic document examination means authenticating documents for the legal community when a question arises about a document's authenticity. Some questions investigated include:

- Who wrote the document[1]?
- Who signed the document?
- Did someone alter a document?
- On what printer, or type of printer, was the document printed?
- Is the stamp produced by ink or on a printer with toner?
- Was the signature added to the document using software?
- Is the email legitimate?
- What software or device was used to create an image?

Many other potential questions may be investigated.

According to the Scientific Working Group for Forensic Document Examination (SWGDOC, www.swgdoc.org), "The forensic document examiner conducts scientific examinations, comparisons,

---

[1] A document can be anything that contains writing. I have examined toilet paper with handwriting and walls containing graffiti.

and analyses of documents in order to: (1) establish genuineness or non-genuineness, or to reveal alterations, additions, or deletions, (2) identify or eliminate persons as the source of handwriting, (3) identify or eliminate the source of machine produced documents, typewriting, or other impression marks, or relative evidence, and (4) preserve and/or restore legibility. They also write technical reports and give expert testimony."

WHAT TYPE OF DOCUMENTS ARE EXAMINED?

Most work performed by document examiners involves analysis of handwriting. Much of the handwriting examination work is to determine the authenticity of signatures. The document examiner may be asked to determine who signed a document. If the person whose name is in the signature did not execute the signature, the document examiner may be asked to discover who wrote the signature.

Black's Law Dictionary Tenth Edition defines *signature* as, "1. A person's name or mark written by that person or at the person's direction 2. *Commercial law*. Any name, mark, or writing used with the intention of authenticating a document. 3. The act of signing something; the handwriting of one's name in one's usual fashion."

In addition to signatures, document examiners review handwritten text on a document.

In one case, I was given several pages of questioned writing and several pages of writing known to have been written by two people. The question was whether one or more writers of the known writing had written the questioned text. The result of the analysis was that one of the writers of the known writing did write the questioned writing.

Figure 1.1 shows the red writing of Joan superimposed over the green questioned writing and the blue writing of the same word written by Mark, superimposed over the green questioned writing. Joan's letter formations, spacing, and other attributes are virtually the same as the questioned writing.

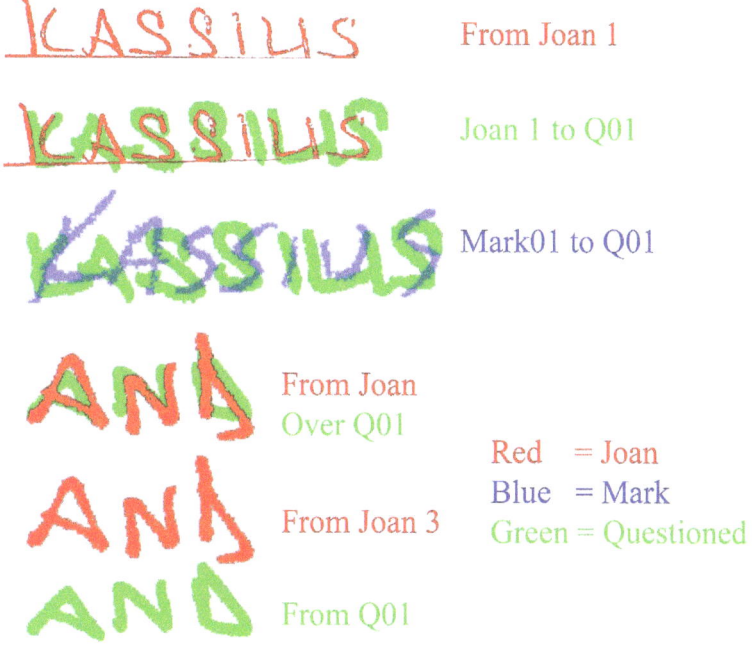

Figure 1.1 Did one of the two people write the document?

Document examiners may determine whether documents were printed on the same printer. In these cases, a microscope may be used to examine the way the letters are formed on the page and what type of printer created the characters on the page. Anomalies produced by the printer are compared.

Document examiners look at the way the pages were printed, such as whether they were printed on a laser, inkjet, wax, or other type of printer. Two documents may look the same to our eyes, yet when examining them under a microscope the type of printer used to create the document becomes apparent.

The document examiner may be able to determine that the same type of printer was used rather than the exact same printer. In cases where the printer causes a repeated anomaly, the exact printer may be identified. In one case, I was able to determine that several documents were printed on the same printer, because the printer always placed a dot of spurious ink at the same location on each page.

TERMINOLOGY USED BY DOCUMENT EXAMINERS

Terminology used by forensic document examiners is defined in legal code, law dictionaries, and standards written by forensic document examiners and managed by standards organizations. ASTM International offered many standards for forensic document examiners. In January, 2017 many of the ASTM standards were retired, then adopted by SWGDOC. In 2012 ASTM dissolved Committee E30.02, forensic document examination. When the standards reached their renewal date they were retired from ASTM.

ASTM standards E1658-04, and E2195-02 and their respective SWGDOC standards, *Terminology Relating to the Examination of Questioned Documents and Standard Terminology for Expressing Conclusions of Forensic Document Examiners*, offer definitions for terms used by forensic document examiners. Both state code and federal code offer definitions applicable to forensic document examiners.

ASTM standard E1732-11b defines terms used in forensic science. This standard applies to all forensic sciences.

In 2016 the Scientific Association of Forensic Examiners (https://safeforensics.org) published updated standards for forensic document examination.

Both the SAFE and SWGDOC standards are included in the National Institute for Standards and Technology (NIST) catalog of recognized standards.

Black's Law Dictionary Tenth Edition defines a *document* as, 1) "Something tangible on which words, symbols or marks are recorded," and 2) "The deeds, agreements, title papers, letters, receipts, and other written instruments used to prove a fact."

In today's environment, documents are also intangible, computer-generated images, such as a scan of a tangible item, an e-mail, a signature written on a digital tablet, a photograph or a report written on a computer.

Many electronic documents are converted into portable document format (PDF) to share the documents across different computer platforms. PDF files are complex documents that can be edited. If proper security is placed onto the document, editing is restricted.

Document examiners must have the skills necessary to examine all these forms of documents.

Written documents

The definition of writing in both Federal Rules of Evidence and California Evidence Code states that writing takes many forms not normally considered by most people. In fact, this book is a writing which takes many forms.

1. It is electronically stored on a computer's hard disc drive
2. It is electronically stored in a computer's memory
3. It is printed on paper
4. It is presented in three e-book formats

These definitions are elaborated in Chapter 2.

Written documents are not always produced using common writing materials. Walls containing graffiti are documents. Some documents are created with mechanical printers, such as an ink jet or toner laser printers and photocopy machines.

A document examiner must be able to distinguish among different forms of mechanical printing.

Some documents have writing executed on digital tablets. These are tablets such as those used in retail stores, some bank loan documents, delivery receipts, and many other applications.

Writing executed on digital tablets presents potential difficulties for the forensic document examiner. The intent of the writing may result in different executions in different situations. When a person signs their name for a loan document on a digital tablet, they will usually write their signature in a normal fashion. When signing a digital tablet at a store, they may write an illegible mark or scrawl. Digital writing tablets are addressed in Chapter 10.

When a document is handwritten on paper, the document includes the paper, the ink used, the toner or ink used by the mechanical printer, and any other marks on the page. All these items can offer clues to the authenticity of a document.

When authenticating handwriting, document examiners need many samples of the suspected writer's writing. The samples are called "exemplars." Often, 20 or more samples of a person's writing are needed. The exemplars are used to determine the variation of the writing. The questioned writing is compared with the exemplars to determine whether it comports with the known writing.

THE NEED FOR A SCIENCE-BASED APPROACH

Document examiners must use a scientifically-based approach to authenticate documents. Failure to use a scientific approach to their work may cause the court to disallow the testimony and/or report.

To qualify as science-based, the approach must provide a methodology that is both repeatable by other examiners and reproducible by the same examiner. The methodology used by the document examiner may be written in the report and/or delivered in testimony at a formal hearing.

Contrary to a common belief of those who are not forensic document examiners, there is no silver bullet methodology. In science, the investigator must be creative. The document examiner must be able to apply generally-accepted methodologies as defined in the standards, then adapt those standards to the requirements of the case at hand to find the proper solution. The document examiner must be able to think beyond the textbook approach. Detective thinking must be applied to generally accepted practices.

A scientifically-based approach reduces potential bias by exploring various aspects of the examination from multiple angles.

For example, when determining whether a person signed a document, both similarities and differences are documented. The reason(s) one set of evidence carries more weight than other evidence must be stated in the report or testimony.

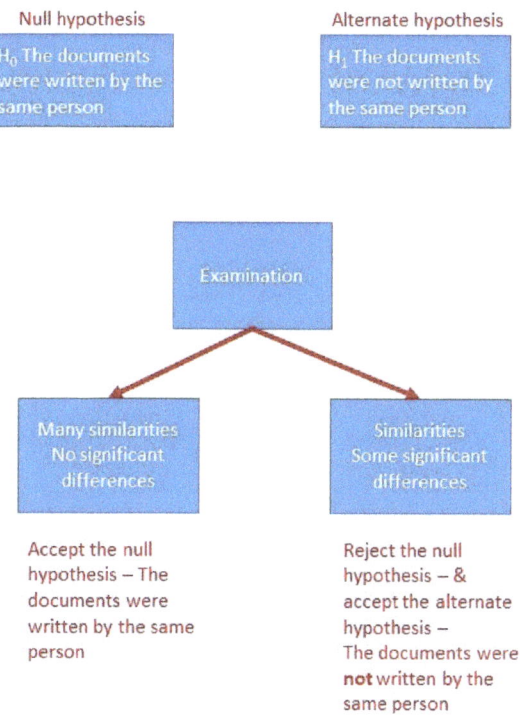

Figure 1.2 How a hypothesis is accepted

A scientific approach means that the document examiner starts with a hypothesis and tries to disprove the hypothesis.

A hypothesis is an assumption that is tested to determine the validity of the assumption.

An examiner may start with a hypothesis that two documents were written by the same person. As an investigator, the examiner looks at the documents and asks, "Can I show they were not written by the same person?"

If there is a way the examiner can say, "These were not written by the same person," the examiner would opine they are not written by the same person. If the examiner cannot show the documents were not written by the same person, then the examiner may say they were written by the same person.

Alternatively, if the evidence does not demonstrate that the document was absolutely written by the same person or not written by the same person, the examiner may give a qualified opinion which leaves room for doubt.

The document examiner may opine "no conclusion" when the evidence is insufficient to opine toward identification or elimination of the writer. Document examiners prove no hypothesis. They can only accept the alternate hypothesis or fail to reject the null hypothesis. See Chapter 3, "Document examiners' opinions" for the full range of opinions defined by the standards.

A science-based approach means that the document examiner explored both evidence that supports the hypothesis and evidence that refutes the hypothesis. The results of each path are given in the report delivered to the client. All evidence must be considered so as not to present an illusion of bias toward one side.

Document examiners must be ready to testify about their opinion in a legal proceeding, such as a deposition, arbitration, or trial. Their opinions must be substantiated with valid reasons and approaches to their work methodology.

If a document examiner walks into a courtroom without valid supporting evidence and says, "I believe this document was written by the same person," or "The person you think wrote it did not write it because that is my opinion," (which happens in practice) this does not does not meet court qualifications as scientific evidence. The method for reaching an opinion must be verifiable, repeatable, and reproducible.

In September 2016, the National Institute of Justice and the United States attorney general issued notice that the word "science" can only be used when quantitative data has been presented with a forensic opinion. In all cases, the phrase "to a reasonable degree of scientific certainty," which is used by some document examiners, is best never used. Nothing in forensic science is certain. The directive states that the term "certainty" can easily mislead or confuse the trier of fact.

AUTHENTICATION OF DOCUMENTS

Black's Law Dictionary Tenth Edition defines *authenticate* as, 1) "To prove the genuineness of (a thing)" and 2) "To render authoritative or authentic, as by attestation or other legal formality."

Document examiners offer evidence to support an opinion regarding the authenticity of documents. The opinion results from examination of all information provided. The document examiner may request additional data from a client when the evidence provided is insufficient to form an opinion in any direction.

As with all scientific disciplines, data is collected then aggregated into information. The information is examined to develop knowledge. From this knowledge, the document examiner develops an opinion.

The opinion may be unqualified, qualified, or fall in the middle as "no conclusion." An unqualified opinion of "identify" means the document examiner believes, based on all evidence provided, the author of the known writing wrote the questioned document. An unqualified opinion of "eliminate" means the evidence is clear that the author of the known writing did not write the questioned document.

A qualified opinion means the evidence tends toward either identify or eliminate, yet stronger evidence is needed. An opinion of no conclusion means that the evidence does not point in either direction.

Even an unqualified opinion leaves the door open for revision should additional evidence surface.

Authentication includes determining whether a document has been altered. Examples of alteration include:

- Letters or numbers may be changed: a 1 may be changed to a 7 or a 4 to a 9 to collect a larger sum of money or alter the date on a document.
- Language may be added to a report to cover an error in a procedure.
- Language may be removed from a will to remove a beneficiary.
- A page of a contract may be retyped to modify terms. The new page may be printed and then inserted into the set of pages.
- A bank check may be chemically washed to remove the payee and amount so a new payee and amount can be inserted.
- Text may be inserted in a record.
- A signature may be added to a document using mechanical or electronical means.

Although not used by all document examiners, modern software such as Adobe Photoshop and Illustrator, and Corel PHOTO-PAINT® make alteration of electronic documents easy. These alterations may be difficult to detect using unaided visual methods.

Discovery of these alterations may require the use of special software for examining digital documents. An expert in digital forensic imaging may have to assist the document examiner to investigate the case.

Chapter 2

Laws for document examination

FEDERAL RULES OF EVIDENCE §1001 OFFERS SEVERAL IMPORTANT DEFINITIONS.

§1001(a) defines *writing*. "A writing consists of letters, words, numbers, or their equivalent set down in any form." Per this definition, the book you are reading is a writing, regardless of whether the format is hardcopy or digital. Document examiners work with documents that are handwritten, typewritten, or created on computers and then printed on a variety of printers. These documents may be signed. All aspects of the document are writings.

§1001(d) defines *original*. "An original of a writing or recording means the writing or recording itself or any *counterpart* [italics added] intended to have the same effect by the person who executed or issued it. For electronically stored information, 'original' means any printout — or other output readable by sight — if it accurately reflects the information. An original of a photograph includes the negative or a print from it."

§1001(e) defines *duplicate*. "A duplicate means a counterpart produced by a mechanical, photographic, chemical, electronic, or other equivalent process or technique that accurately reproduces the original."

The difference between an original and a duplicate appears to be the intent of use. As an example,

1. A business person sends a contract to a client as an attachment to an email.
2. The client prints the contract.
3. The client signs the contract.
4. The client scans the signed contract to a PDF.
5. The client sends the PDF to the original business person.
6. The business person accepts the signed PDF as a negotiated contract.
7. The business person prints the PDF.
8. The business person stores the contract in a file cabinet.

Based on the definitions of *original* and *duplicate*, for the business person, the printed contract placed into the file cabinet is probably the duplicate while the PDF is an original. For the client, the contract signed by the client is an original and the PDF is a duplicate.

§1002 states, "An original writing, recording, or photograph is required in order to prove its content unless these rules or a federal statute provides otherwise."

The SAFE and SWGDOC standards for handwriting identification require examination of the original document when the original is available. The standards do not define "original."

Typically, a document examiner interprets "original" to mean a page on which writing was executed on the page in question. All other images of the page are treated as duplicates, regardless of the intent of the holder of the document.

Searching the glossaries of document examination text books and standards, I discovered only one citation that defines "original document." The book *Forgery* by Kenneth Raines defines, "original document – A created document; not a copy."

CALIFORNIA EVIDENCE CODE

State jurisdictions offer terminology important for forensic document examiners. Many terms are similar to those in the Federal Rules of Evidence. Often the federal definitions are elaborated in the state definitions. These definitions are from the California Evidence Code. Check your state's code for local definitions.

California Evidence Code §1400: "*Authentication* of a writing means (a) the introduction of evidence sufficient to sustain a finding that it is the writing that the proponent of the evidence claims it is or (b) the establishment of such facts by any other means provided by law."

California Evidence Code §1418: "*The genuineness of a writing*, or lack thereof, may be proved by comparison made by an expert witness with writing (a) which the court finds was admitted or treated as genuine by a party against whom the evidence is offered or (b) otherwise proved to be genuine to the satisfaction of the court."

California Evidence Code §250: "'*Writing*' means handwriting, typewriting, printing, photostating, photographing, photocopying, transmitting by electronic mail or facsimile, and every other means of recording upon any tangible thing, any form of communication or representation, including letters, words, pictures, sounds, or symbols, or combinations thereof, and any record thereby created, regardless of the manner in which the record has been stored."

Although California Evidence Code §250 is more detailed than Federal Rules of Evidence §1001(a), both define that a writing is more than that which is physically produced.

Black's Law Dictionary Tenth Edition defines a *document* as, "Something tangible on which words, symbols, or marks are recorded." Therefore, a document is a writing.

Texas Rules of Evidence
Rule 1001: Definitions

(a) A "writing" consists of letters, words, numbers, or their equivalent set down in any form.

(d) An "original" of a writing or recording means the writing or recording itself or any counterpart intended to have the same effect by the person who executed or issued it. For electronically stored information, "original" means any printout—or other output readable by sight—if it accurately reflects the information. An "original" of a photograph includes the negative or a print from it.

(e) A "duplicate" means a counterpart produced by a mechanical, photographic, chemical, electronic, or other equivalent process or technique that accurately reproduces the original.

Louisiana Code of Evidence
Article 1001: Definitions

(1) Writings and recordings. "Writings" and "recordings" consist of letters, words, numbers, sounds, or their equivalent, set down by handwriting, typewriting, printing, photostating, photographing, magnetic impulse, mechanical or electronic recording, or other form of data compilation.

(3) Original. An "original" of a writing or recording is the writing or recording itself or any counterpart intended to have the same effect by a person executing or issuing it. An "original" of a photograph includes the negative or any print therefrom. If data are stored in or copied onto a computer

or similar device, including any portable or hand-held computer or electronic storage device, any printout or other output readable by sight, shown to reflect the data accurately, is an "original".

(5) Duplicate. A "duplicate" is a counterpart produced by the same impression as the original, or from the same matrix, or by means of photography, including enlargements and miniatures, or by mechanical or electronic re-recording, or electronic imaging, or by chemical reproduction, or by an optical disk imaging system, or by other equivalent techniques, which accurately reproduces the original."

THE LAW OF EXPERT TESTIMONY
Frye v. United States

Document examiners must understand the law pertaining to providing expert testimony. In 1923, Frye v. United States, 293 F. 1013 (D.C. Cir. *1923*), developed law regarding the admissibility of expert testimony.

The Frye case establishes that experts must use generally-accepted practices in the industry when performing scientific examinations. The Frye Court wrote, "while courts will go a long way in admitting expert testimony deduced from a well-recognized scientific principle or discovery, the thing from which the deduction is made must be sufficiently established to have gained general acceptance in the particular field in which it belongs."

Daubert v. Merrell Dow Pharmaceuticals

The 1993, Daubert v. Merrell Dow Pharmaceuticals (92-102), 509 U.S. 579 (1993) changed the requirements for expert testimony in federal court in Rule 702 of the Federal Rules of Evidence.

Many states have adopted the Daubert approach, which makes the judge the gatekeeper who decides whether an expert may testify.

The intent is to keep "junk science" out of the courtroom. Daubert established a test establishing the validity of the methodology used:

- Empirical testing: The theory or technique must be falsifiable, refutable, and testable.
- Subjected to peer review and publication.
- Known or potential error rate for the methodology used.
- The existence and maintenance of standards and controls concerning operating the methodology.
- Degree to which the theory and technique are generally accepted by a relevant scientific community.

In the Daubert opinion the Court wrote,

"(c) Faced with a proffer of expert scientific testimony under Rule 702, the trial judge, pursuant to Rule 104(a), must make a preliminary assessment of whether the testimony's underlying reasoning or methodology is scientifically valid and properly can be applied to the facts at issue. Many considerations will bear on the inquiry, including whether the theory or technique in question can be (and has been) tested, whether it has been subjected to peer review and publication, its known or potential error rate and the existence and maintenance of standards controlling its operation, and whether it has attracted widespread acceptance within a relevant scientific community. The inquiry is a flexible one, and its focus must be solely on principles and methodology, not on the conclusions that they generate."

Additional Supreme Court cases

In the 1995 United States v. Starzecpyzel, 93 Cr 553 (LMM), 880 Fed.Sup. 1027 (S Dist N.Y. 1995), the court determined document examiners are "skilled experts" rather than scientists. The Daubert standard was not applied to forensic document examiners.

In 1997 in the Kumho Tire Co. v. Carmichael, 526 U.S. 137 (1999), the United States Supreme Court applied the Daubert standard to all expert testimony, not just testimony from scientists. Therefore, the Daubert tests apply to forensic document examiners.

Does Frye apply to forensic document examiners?

Because the Starzecpyzel Court ruled that document examiners are "skilled experts" rather than scientists, the Frye standard may not apply to forensic document examiners. Frye only applies to, "scientific principle or discovery." The determination may depend on whether "scientific" modifies "discovery." If "scientific" does not modify "discovery," Frye would apply to document examiners.

In trial, a judge reminded me that Frye does not apply to my discipline because document examiners are not scientists. Not all judges interpret Frye in this manner. Chapter 13 includes a more detailed discussion about Frye.

Chapter 3

Standards for forensic document examiners

In 1997 the Federal Bureau of Investigation (FBI) sponsored the Scientific Working Group for Document Examination (SWGDOC, www.swgdoc.org). This working group developed standards for document examiners to follow to be in compliance with best practices.

The standards are guidance documents for document examiners rather than standards codified for regulated industries such as pharmaceutical, medical devices, and banking. Document examiners are not audited to determine whether they have standard operating procedures in place to implement the standards. Regulated industries such as banking, pharmaceutical, medical device, food handling, etc. are audited to ensure adherence to industry standards.

Later these standards were adopted by ASTM International (www.astm.org) under committee E30.02. In 2012 Committee E30.02 was dissolved and the standards were taken back by SWGDOC. ASTM moved the document examination standards to committee E30.90. As the ASTM standards expire they are not being renewed by ASTM. The ASTM and SWGDOC standards are identical.

In 2013 the United States Congress stopped funding for most forensic Scientific Working Groups in favor of the Organization of Scientific Area Committees (OSAC). OSAC is a joint effort between the United States Department of Justice and National Institute of Standards and Technology. The objective of OSAC is to create a uniform approach to forensic disciplines. Five committees are subdivided into 31 subcommittees. Forensic document examination is a subcommittee of the Physics/Pattern Recognition Committee.

Committee members are from laboratories staffed by government forensics practitioners, private forensics practitioners, and academics. Committees also have members from law enforcement. The objective is to have representation from all aspects of each of the 31 forensics disciplines. The private sector represents 16 percent of the membership, academic 17 percent, and government 65 percent. Federally funded research and development centers comprise the final 2 percent of OSAC membership.

The SWGDOC Standard for Minimum Training Requirements for Forensic Document Examiners offers guidance for the minimum educational requirements for document examiners. The standards define a base methodology for examination of documents. In 2016 Dr. Carolyne Bird and Dr. Bryan Found from Australia published a 10-step procedure for examination of handwritten documents: *The Modular Forensic Handwriting Method 2016 Version*. The methodology is well tested and validated.

If a document examiner follows the SAFE, SWGDOC, or Australian methodology, the document examiner is following a generally accepted practice for the discipline.

In August, 2016, the Scientific Association of Forensic Examiners published a set of five standards for forensic document examiners. These standards have been accepted and published by the National Institute of Standards and Technology (NIST) for the catalog of standards.

THE SAFE STANDARDS
Title of Standard
- SAFE Handwriting Examination Standard
- SAFE Report Language Standard
- SAFE Reporting Opinions Standard for Handwriting Examination
- SAFE Request Writing Standard
- SAFE Scope of Work Standard

THE SWGDOC STANDARDS
Title of Standard
- SWGDOC Standard for Scope of Work of Forensic Document Examiners
- SWGDOC Standard for Test Methods for Forensic Writing Ink Comparison
- SWGDOC Standard Terminology for Expressing Conclusions for Forensic Document Examiners
- SWGDOC Standard for Writing Ink Comparison
- SWGDOC Standard Terminology Relating to the Examination of Questioned Documents
- SWGDOC Standard for Examination of Mechanical Checkwriter Impressions
- SWGDOC Standard for Examination of Dry Seal Impressions
- SWGDOC Standard for Examination of Fracture Patterns and Paper Fiber Impressions on Single-Strike Film Ribbons for Typed Text
- Standard Guide SWGDOC Standard de for Physical Match of Paper Cuts, Tears and Perforations in Forensic Document Examination
- SWGDOC Standard for Examination of Rubber Stamp Impressions

- Standard SWGDOC Standard Guide for Examination of Handwritten Items
- SWGDOC Standard for Indentation Examinations
- SWGDOC Standard for Non-Destructive Examination of Paper
- SWGDOC Standard for Examination of Altered Documents
- SWGDOC Standard for Minimum Training Requirements for Forensic Document Examiners
- SWGDOC Standard for Examination of Documents Produced With Liquid Ink Jet Technology
- SWGDOC Standard for Examination of Documents Produced With Toner Technology
- SWGDOC Standard for Examination of Typewritten Items
- SWGDOC Standard for Preservation of Charred Documents
- SWGDOC Standard for Preservation of Liquid Soaked Documents
- Standard Practice for Use of Image Capture and Storage Technology in Forensic Document Examination

HUBER & HEDRICK[2] PROPOSED 21 ELEMENTS FOR DISCRIMINATION OF HANDWRITING.

1. Arrangement
2. Class of allograph (cursive, manuscript, printing, composite)
3. Connections (inter-word and intra-word)
4. Designs of allographs and their construction
5. Dimensions
6. Slant and slope
7. Spacings (inter-word and intra-word)
8. Abbreviations
9. Alignment

[2] Huber, A. M. & Hedrick, R. *Handwriting Identification: Facts and Fundamentals.* (CRC Press, Boca Raton, 1999) pp. 91 - 139.

10. Commencements and terminations
11. Diacritics and punctuations (presence, style and location)
12. Embellishments
13. Legibility or writing quality
14. Line continuity
15. Line quality
16. Pen control
17. Writing movement
18. Consistency or natural variation
19. Persistency
20. Lateral Expansion
21. Word proportions

These attributes are discussed in Chapter 5.

DOCUMENT EXAMINERS' OPINIONS

The SAFE Reporting Opinions Standard for Handwriting Examination defines seven qualitative terms used by document examiners to express their opinions

The SWGDOC Standard defines nine qualitative terms used by document examiners to express their opinions (see Figure 3.1).

Document examiners' opinions are expressed in qualified or unqualified terms. In both standards, the unqualified opinions are *identify* and *eliminate*. In the SAFE standard, the qualified opinions are *probably did write, strong probability did write, probably did not write,* and *strong probability did write*.

In the SWGDOC standard the qualified opinions are: *indications, probably,* and *strong probability* in each direction from the center. "No conclusion" is in the middle because this means the evidence does not point in either direction.

Identify means the document examiner is convinced that the writer of the known writing is the writer of the questioned writing. Elimination means the document examiner is convinced that the writer of the known writing is not the writer of the questioned writing. Identify

Figure 3.1 SWGDOC Document Examiner's Opinions

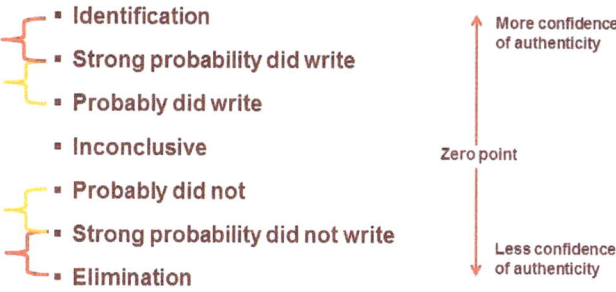

Figure 3.2 SAFE Document Examiner's Opinions

and eliminate retain the option that if new evidence is presented that contradicts the existing evidence, the opinion may change. Neither holds a 100% certainty.

These terms I will also apply to determining the authenticity of a document. Identification means the document examiner is convinced that the document is authentic. Elimination means the document examiner is convinced that the document is not authentic.

Care must be taken when offering an unqualified opinion. The opinions affect people's lives. For this reason, authorities state that we need enough exemplars to perform the examination of handwriting or documents.

Determining variability of the handwriting requires enough exemplars to know how a person writes. No specific number of exemplars is needed. The answer to the required quantity of exemplars is, "a sufficient number to draw a valid opinion."

Measurement of the writing to determine the variability requires at least 12 exemplars. Additional exemplars strengthen the assessment of the variability. A much stronger opinion can be reached from a quantitative perspective when 30 or more exemplars have been measured.

The document examiner's responsibility is to continue requesting additional exemplars until a valid opinion can be reached. Otherwise, an inconclusive opinion may be the correct opinion.

Initially, a qualified opinion may result when the data is not sufficient to resolve all differences between the known writing and the questioned writing. When this occurs, the document examiner asks the client to look for additional exemplars to resolve the differences.

Too many exemplars are better than too few. Providing too few exemplars increases the cost of the examination since the document examiner must stop and then restart the analysis when additional exemplars are delivered.

The provenance of the exemplars is not always known. There are times I have refused to use documents provided as known examples of a person's writing. Examples are pages of writing without a signature, cards written to a person, or other documents for which the source cannot be verified.

Even notarized documents may not be authentic. In a trial, a notary testified that the signature on a document was not hers, yet the stamp was hers. The photocopied document was probably made by using software to insert a copy of her stamp onto the document, print the false document, and then have a forger write her name into the signature location. A photocopy of the page was made and presented as a photocopy of a legitimate document.

Fewer exemplars may be needed for the opinion, identify than for the opinion eliminate. This is because the writing between the known and questioned documents may be so similar. Without significant differences, the chance of two people having written the documents is very small. Elimination requires enough samples to determine whether features in the questioned writing also appear in the known writing.

At a trial to determine the authenticity of a holographic will, the opposing examiner had two exemplars. Based on these, the opposing examiner opined the decedent had not authored the will.

I had more than 20 exemplars. I could show features of the questioned writing appearing in the known writing. The opposing examiner stated that these features of the questioned writing did not appear in the known writing. My opinion was that there was a strong probability the decedent wrote the will. The court agreed with my opinion. The difference was the number of exemplars examined by each examiner.

In the Case United States v. LeBeau, 5:14-CR-50048-KES (D.S.D. Jun. 10, 2015), the Court rejected the results presented by the defense's document examiner because only one exemplar was used for comparison. The document examiner eliminated the suspect as the author of the questioned document.

"The fact that [defense's document examiner's] opinion relied upon one document which purported to be the "known" signature for comparison purposes, without requiring additional known signatures and the context in which they were given, renders her testimony less credible. Her analysis and opinions entirely hinge on whether she received an accurate "known" signature from Gers. Her opinions are further undermined by the fact that she believes it highly probable that Lyle Tolsma also signed Gerald LeBeau's signature. Even from the untrained eye of this court, there is striking similarity from Gers LeBeau's signature on Exhibit 11 and Gers LeBeau's signature on Exhibit 15. It also bears mentioning that Gers signed the Permission to Search form (Exhibit 11) while he was in handcuffs. Approximately 6 hours later, Gers signed the Inmate Property Orientation Sheet. Notably, Agent Tolsma did not accompany Gers to the jail or was present when Gers signed this form.

The court rejects the testimony of [defense's document examiner] and determines that based on the testimony of [plaintiff's document examiners], the consent form was signed by Gers LeBeau."

The names of the document examiners have been removed for this book.

Chapter 4

Document examiners' tools

A good indication of the quality of a document examiner is the tools, and the quality of the tools they use to examine documents. Always ask your prospective examiner for a list of tools they use. You will find significant differences among examiners.

Figure 4.1 Digital microscope

A *digital microscope* is used to capture an enlarged image into a computer. An example of a high quality digital microscope is called MiScope from Zarbeco in New Jersey (Figure 4.1). The microscope has many built-in capabilities such as variable magnification, software to capture the image, built-in infrared and ultraviolet light lamps, etc. Use of alternate light sources is used to differentiate inks or discover alterations to the document. Less expensive digital microscopes are available. They may not offer the same resolution or capabilities as the MiScope. The resolution of the MiScope is 2.0 megapixels.

An *optical stereo microscope* (Figure 4.2) provides a magnified three-dimensional look at an image. The three-dimensional view enables the document examiner to see depth. This tool makes it possible to observe aspects of the writing such as indentation of the stroke on the page, or line crossings.

Figure 4.2 Optical microscope

A trinocular version permits attaching a camera onto the third tube on top to photograph the image seen through the eyepieces. When a digital camera is attached, the image can be sent directly to the computer.

The digital camera is the small black box on top of the trinocular tube in the photo. There is a wire from the camera to a USB connector on the computer. The computer has software to capture the image from the camera and display it on the screen. The image can be stored on the computer.

Figure 4.3 Viewing scope

Infrared and Ultraviolet viewing scopes, such as a Find-R-Scope, enable viewing a document with alternative light sources outside the visibility of the human eye. Filters of different wavelengths may be attached to the viewing scopes to see different aspects of the document. These are often used to determine whether a document has been altered.

Figure 4.4 Loupe

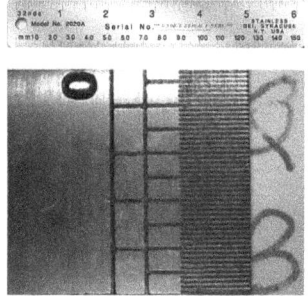

Figure 4.5 Ruler

A *Loupe* (Figure 4.4) is a small magnifier used to examine a portion of a document. It is a small portable microscope with one eyepiece, often used by jewelers. The image is not typically photographed through a loupe. Loupes come in various magnification levels, such as 10x, 15x, 20x.

A *NIST* (National Institute for Standards and Technology) *Standard Ruler* (Figure 4.5) is a specially calibrated metal ruler. The ruler has increments as small as 1/100 inch. The examiner places the ruler under a loupe or microscope to read the length being measured.

The NIST standard ruler is precise at 68 degrees Fahrenheit (20 degrees Celsius). The bottom image in Figure 4.5 shows a magnification of a ruler adjacent to letters which are being measured. The measurement is an approximation since the precision is based on the viewing angle and the observer's ability to read the correct mark on the ruler. Since the measurement is rounded to the closest ruler marking, rounding error will occur. I prefer to use Photoshop to make my measurements (see Figure 4.6) because it offers better accuracy.

Adobe Photoshop® software is a powerful tool used to compare writing, determine alterations, examine digital images and perform many other functions. Photoshop enables cutting a section of writing on one document and overlaying the cut section onto a similar writing on another document. This is superior to the naked eye, which many document examiners rely on, when determining

Figure 4.6 Photoshop

whether a character or set of characters in the questioned writing is similar to the same set of characters in known writing. Photoshop is used to examine scanned images of ink and documents.

Photoshop contains a very precise measuring tool. This tool is used to measure the length and angle of portions of the writing. These measurements are more precise than a ruler or protractor.

Photoshop is also used to create demonstrative exhibits for reports and courtroom testimony.

Figure 4.7 Computer

A *Computer* (Figure 4.7) is used to store all digital images, write reports, create demonstrative exhibits, etc. A laptop computer enables the document examiner to examine documents outside the document examiner's laboratory. The portable digital microscope, flatbed scanner and other equipment can be attached to capture the images of the documents directly to the computer for examination.

Figure 4.8 Flatbed scanner

A *Flatbed scanner* (Figure 4.8) is used to scan documents into the computer. Once the documents are stored in the computer, they can be examined using Photoshop. This enables the examiner to work with the document without concern of harming the source document.

A flatbed scanner is used rather than a sheet-fed scanner. A sheet-fed scanner uses wheels to pull the document across the scanning device. The wheels can potentially mark or damage the document. In a flatbed scanner, the document is placed onto glass. No moving parts touch the document. A scanner uses software installed on the computer. Software instructs the scanner regarding the desired resolution, detail, type of file to save the image, and many other attributes.

Figure 4.9 ESDA

An *Electrostatic detection device* (Figure 4.9) is used to detect indented writing. The device shown here is an Electrostatic Detection Device (ESDA), manufactured by Foster and Freeman from England. Indented writing is writing that appears on the page below the page on which a person has written (on a pad or stack of paper).

The indented writing is an impression caused by the pressure of the pen on the page above. Indented writing shows the document examiner what was written on the page above. The electrostatic detection device can sometimes show impressions of what was written on several pages above. This device can also be used to assist with solving the problem of which line in the writing was drawn first.

Figure 4.10 VSC

The *video spectral comparator* (VSC) (Figure 4.10) is an expensive piece of equipment manufactured by Foster and Freeman. The VSC uses infrared and ultraviolet light to examine a document. VSCs are useful to help solve the line crossing problem, erasures, differentiation of inks, and chemical alterations of documents.

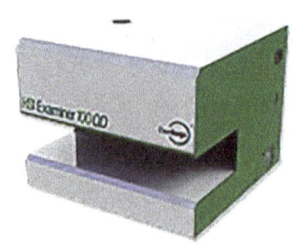

Figure 4.11 HSI Examiner

Figure 4.12 Digital camera

Hyperspectral imaging system Video Spectral Comparator HSI Examiner™ 100 QD (Figure 4.11). The HSI is manufactured by ChemImage from Pittsburgh, Pennsylvania. This equipment is typically used by government laboratories for authentication of government documents such as passports, driver's licenses, etc. The price starts around $90,000 USD.

Most digital cameras (Figure 4.12) have a filter that eliminates the infrared light, which is invisible to the human eye. Companies can remove the infrared filter from the camera. This is valuable for photographing documents in various wavelengths of infrared light.

The visible light spectrum is approximately 400 nm - 700 nm (nm = nanometers) frequency. Many inks appear to be the same color to the human eye. The wavelength frequency of infrared light is between approximately 700 - 1000 nm.

Special filters are placed onto the camera's lens. The filters allow the camera to "see" the infrared light at the frequency specified for the filter. The digital camera's receptors then capture the image. A film camera requires film that is sensitive to infrared light.

Later, in Chapter 9, images taken using infrared filters on the camera and through the digital microscope are examined. Although the digital camera can be a substitute for the VSC or HSI, the VSC and HSI are sensitive to more frequencies of infrared than the camera.

Digital calipers (example in Figure 4.13 is manufactured by Mitutoyo) are used to measure the thickness of paper, the height of mechanically printed characters, the distance between staple holes, and other applications.

One instance where this is valuable is when the document examiner needs to determine whether a page in a document may have been taken from a different ream of paper than the rest of the pages in a document. Since most paper used in printers and photocopy machines is the same weight (typically 20 pounds), the calipers may not be useful to determine whether multiple pages of paper originated from the same lot.

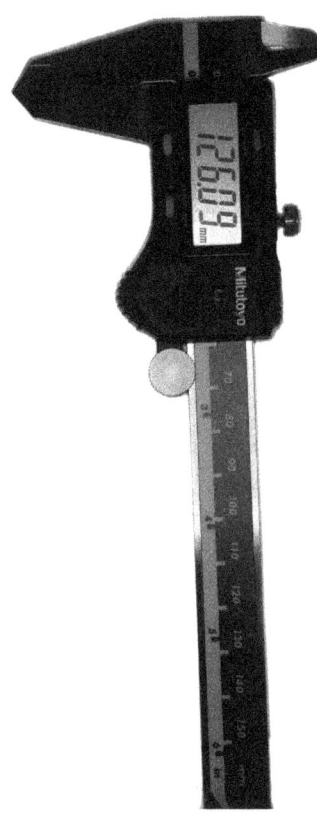

Figure 4.13 Calipers

The document examiner uses gloves when handling original documents. Human hands have oils which can contaminate documents. Wearing proper gloves is especially important if the document is to be examined for fingerprints. The document examiner does not want to add their fingerprints to the document. Nitrile gloves are the best gloves since the nitrile does not pass oils through the material. Cotton and other fiber-based gloves have the potential to pass skin oil through to the paper.

Chapter 5

Each assignment is a project

A *project* is defined in the Guide to the Project Management Body of Knowledge Fifth Edition as, "A temporary endeavor undertaken to create a unique product, service, or result."[3] Each case worked by a forensic document examiner is unique. The result is an opinion and/or a report describing the methodology used to culminate in the opinion.

Although the focus of examinations may be similar, such as authenticating a signature or determining whether a document has been altered, the techniques applied may differ. An analogy is that the English language has 26 characters in the alphabet and a finite number of words in the language. The way the letters are arranged yields different words, and the order in which the words are arranged yields different messages. For example, the words *may* and *yam* have the same letters yet very different meanings.

Similarly, defined steps may be used across examinations, yet the order will differ depending upon the case. In some cases, the

---

[3] Project Management Institute. (2013). *A Guide to the project management body of knowledge*. Project Management Institute: Newtown Square.

examiner may scan the documents first, followed by the microscopic examination. In other cases, the examiner may use the microscope before scanning the document.

T.S. Eliot (1943) wrote, "We shall not cease from exploration and the end of all our exploring will be to arrive where we started and know the place for the first time."[4] Document examiners are explorers. Every time a document examiner works on a case, the material is new. The questioned writing differs from any other case. The known writing usually differs from any other case. The physical documents usually differ completely from any other case. The document examiner must first examine the evidence received to plan the strategy for working the case.

Occasionally when a case is received, a client will describe the case as "a slam dunk," "simple, even a first grader can see the difference," etc. To the layperson, the answer whether a person wrote a document often appears obvious.

The trained document examiner must look beyond the obvious. As an investigator, the document examiner sometimes works on a case and then puts it aside for a while before returning with a fresh perspective. This process provides the document examiner the ability to determine whether the initial results are correct. It is a good method of reducing bias. If the second examination results in a different result, the document examiner must resolve the differences.

I had a case that my client attorney said would be simple. My first opinion on the case was, "no conclusion." The exemplars he had provided were insufficient to determine whether the decedent had executed the signature on the will. I needed additional exemplars to solve the case.

My client provided many more examples of the decedent's writing. With the additional data my investigation eventually yielded an opinion in the case, which turned out to be quite complex.

---

[4] Eliot, T. S. (1943). *Little Gidding in Four Quartets.* Harcourt: San Diego.

Document examiners cannot say, "I've seen this before so I know the answer." It's never that simple. Each case is a project because the evidence provided is different and the scope is different. Therefore, the work performed and the results are unique for each case.

In another case, the attorney client provided more than 30 exemplars of the decedent's signature. The question asked was, "Did the decedent sign the will?" Examination of the decedent's signature showed that he substantially varied his signature from writing to writing. The questioned signature was at the extreme of the variability of the known writing. The resultant opinion was "no conclusion." The attorney's client did not want to spend additional money for my trip to the courthouse to examine the original will or perform additional work with more exemplars.

MATHEMATICS AND PROBABILITY THEORY IN DOCUMENT EXAMINATION

Ordway Hilton wrote, "We are not making our conclusion any more scientific or accurate by resorting to mathematics or probability theory."[5] I am refuting Hilton's statement in this book.

Mathematics and probability theory give us an additional basis on which to substantiate an opinion. The basis of handwriting identification is for the document examiner to understand the variability of a person's writing. Variability is a mathematical concept. By applying the mathematics of variability to the handwriting, a document examiner can better obtain understanding about how to proceed with the investigation. The result determines whether the questioned writing may have come from the same set of writing as the known writing.

ASTM Standard 444 (also SWGDOC Standard 444), Scope of Work for Forensic Document Examiners states, "Questions about

---

[5] Hilton, O. (1995). The relationship of mathematical probability to the handwriting identification problem. International Journal of Forensic Document Examiners. (1)3, 224-229.

documents are answered through . . . education specific to forensic document examination as well as from a number of other fields, such as the physical sciences, mathematics, . . ."

Dr. Sargur Srihari at State University of New York at Buffalo said that we must develop a scientific basis that is based on error rates. Srihari led a team to develop computer software for the United States Postal Service for handwriting identification based on a statistical approach. The software uses digital image processing and pattern recognition to identify writers. Based upon Srihari's work, much additional research has been conducted to identify writers using statistically based analysis.

The International Graphonomics Society and the Institute of Electrical and Electronic Engineers (IEEE) Special Interest Group on Pattern Recognition publish substantial research using computers and statistical analysis for writer identification.

Chapter 6

Examination of handwriting

Handwriting is often referred to as *brain writing* because it is a complex neuromotor interaction where the brain tells the muscles how to move the arm and hand to write. Writing is performed with the entire body. The hand is merely the part of the body that holds the writing instrument.

In 1929 British researcher, Robert Saudek, published the book *Experiments With Handwriting*. A portion of his research examines the difference in handwriting of soldiers from World War I who lost their primary arm due to battle injuries. Saudek wanted to find whether the handwriting differed when the soldier learned to write with the other hand. He discovered that although there are differences, eventually the handwriting in the new hand resembled the earlier writing with the primary hand.

Exemplars versus questioned documents

Document examiners use two sets of documents for handwriting identification. The known documents, called *exemplars*, are written by the person whose writing is being compared with the questioned document. The questioned document is the document the examiner will analyze to determine its authenticity. ASTM Standard E1732-17, *Standard Terminology Relating To Forensic Science*, defines *exemplar*: "a specimen of physical evidence of known origin."

The document examiner can generally state a stronger opinion when they obtain a larger number of known documents. This is because when consistent attributes are seen across multiple writing sessions, the examiner can be sure this is a common feature of the person's writing.

Also, with more exemplars, unusual attributes of the person's writing are more likely to be discovered. These unusual attributes may occur only occasionally. When the attributes occur infrequently, there is a chance they will be missed in a small sample. If the unusual attribute appears in the questioned document, a small sample may cause the document examiner to make an erroneous opinion toward elimination.

Examination Procedure

Handwriting examination is a comparative analysis. It falls within the pattern recognition forensic disciplines such as the examination of fingerprints, footwear impressions, tire impressions, tool marks, and firearms.

The document examiner must be careful to not find patterns that do not exist. A difficulty with a purely subjective approach to pattern recognition disciplines is that the methodology is not necessarily repeatable or reproducible. A more objective methodology is required to support an opinion.

The general procedure for examination of handwriting is described in the *Modular Forensic Handwriting Method*. The forensic document examiner analyzes the questioned document to find the anomalies in the writing and/or signature. These identifying unique attributes are documented. Next the exemplars are studied to determine the common attributes of the person's known handwriting. The identifying unique attributes of the known writing are then documented. The unique identifying attributes in the questioned writing are compared with those in the known writing. The examiner then determines whether those common, unique attributes are present in the both the questioned writing and known writing.

The attributes discovered by the skilled document examiner are substantially more detailed than the overall structure of the writing. Attributes such as spacing, relative size of letters, starts and stops within the writing, pressure of the writing, and many others are examined. As stated in chapter 3, Huber and Hedrick identified twenty-one attributes of handwriting which a document examiner should examine. Not all attributes will always be present in the writing. As an example, the signature may not use diacritics or abbreviations.

Initial questions the document examiner must ask and answer are:

1. Are the exemplars of sufficient quality for examination?
2. Is the questioned writing of sufficient quality for examination?
3. Are there are enough exemplars for comparison?

If the answer to each question is yes, the document examiner can proceed with the examination. If the quality of the exemplars is not sufficient, the document examiner will request new exemplars to obtain exemplars of sufficient quality for examination.

If the questioned writing or the known writing is of insufficient quality for examination, the document examiner will report this information to the client. The document examiner will then stop the work.

The next questions the document examiner seeks to answer are:

1. Were all the exemplars written by the same person?
2. Was the questioned writing written by the same person who wrote the exemplars?

COLLECTION OF EXEMPLARS

ASTM Standard E1732-12, *Standard Terminology Relating to Forensic Science* (the standard is not specific to forensic document examination), defines *exemplar* as, "a specimen of physical evidence of known origin." The standard is not specific for document examination. For handwriting examination, exemplars are the samples known to have been written by a person whose writing is being compared with the questioned (disputed) writing. The document examiner works under the assumption the exemplars were written by the person who allegedly wrote them. This is an assumption because the document examiner did not observe the person executing the writing.

At times I have rejected exemplars because there is no indication of the provenance of the writing.

Handwriting can be printed, manuscript, cursive, or mixed print and cursive. Handwritten text is best compared with handwritten text: cursive to cursive, printed to printed. Signatures are best compared with signatures. Many people write their signatures differently from the way they write text. Handwritten text is generally not compared with signatures.

Compare similar forms of handwriting

Document examiners typically will not compare a person's initials with the person's signature. The reason is many people write their initials differently from the way they write a signature. The reason for this is the letter sequence when writing initials differs from the letter sequence when writing the signature.

The document examiner may need to compare signatures with handwritten text due to lack of signatures for comparison. An opinion toward identification of the writer may be determined when the writer uses the same style of writing for text and signatures. An opinion toward elimination of the writer is impossible because the writer may sign their name differently from the way they write text. A possible reason for the difference is signatures are written so frequently they are often illegible. Signatures are written more from habit than is general course of business writing. The content of a signature does not change whereas the general course of business writing is unique to the situation. When people write text they generally want the text to be legible so more care is taken in the writing.

When comparing handwriting, the source handwriting is best when it is the same type of handwriting as the questioned handwriting. Normal course of business writing such as a check, deed, contract or other legal document is needed to compare with writing on a legal document. A letter or card to a friend or family requires other informal writing. People tend to write differently, especially a signature, in different circumstances.

At a presentation by neurologist Dr. Evelyne Pannetier during the 2011 National Association of Document Examiners conference in Montreal, Dr. Pannetier described how we write differently depending whether we are writing freely, taking dictation or copying.

She said the reason is that different parts of the brain are involved in the neuro-motor coordination for different situations. When taking request exemplars, the document examiner requests many iterations of writing. The later writing becomes more natural than the first iterations. Details about request exemplars are described later in this chapter.

Types of exemplars

Exemplars fall into two primary categories: 1) Existing writing exemplars, and 2) request exemplars.

People often write the same character differently depending on the location of the character in the word or character sequence.

Existing writing exemplars

Usually the document examiner receives exemplars of a person's signature or handwriting. Unless the document examiner sees the person execute the writing, only the word of the person supplying the writing is used to ascertain the writing was executed by the named person. I always include a statement in the report that an assumption of the examination is the handwriting is that of the person who allegedly executed the handwriting.

Exemplars should be written contemporaneously to the date of the questioned signature. Most document examiners ask for exemplars within 2 or 3 years prior to the date of the questioned signature. Signatures after the questioned signature are acceptable yet are often given less credence than prior signatures. The reason is if the suspect intentionally changed their signature after writing the signature, authentication may be more difficult.

Collecting exemplars that span the date of the questioned signature is valuable. When the exemplars span the date of the questioned writing, the document examiner can determine whether the writing remained consistent or whether there were significant changes in the writing. When the writing is consistent across the questioned date, an expectation is that if the author of the exemplars wrote the questioned writing, the questioned writing will present the same characteristics as the exemplars. If the writer of the exemplars did not write the questioned writing; the questioned writing will deviate from the exemplars.

Existing writing exemplars are found in many locations. Common sources of signatures are contracts, deeds, hospital records, and checks. Your document examiner can suggest sources for handwriting exemplars.

Bank checks may not provide adequate quality exemplars. The reason is that since 2005, the banks have been scanning the checks then shredding them. Often times the checks are presented to a customer with 10 or 12 checks reduced onto a page. The banks scan the checks at relatively low resolution which fails to image the details of writing. When the images are reduced even more of the detail is removed. The checks are usually provided to the customer in PDF format. When clients present check images to me, I asked them to request one check per page then send the PDF document to me. This would be considered the best quality presentation of the check. If the client prints the PDF then sends the printed image to me, there is an opportunity for even more degradation of the image of the writing. The PDF can be read directly into Photoshop where the resolution can be enhanced. The enhanced resolution enables the document examiner to enlarge the image without distortion so the writing can be examined.

Potential problems with photocopy exemplars
Using the document with ink writing is always best as this shows the detailed anomalies of the source document. Photocopies often fail to copy all the details, especially details of handwriting. Notice the light lead-in stroke on the letter a in the ink version. The photocopy does not show this attribute of the writing. Photocopies are also not exact copies of the source document. Photocopy machines

Figure 6.1 Example of problem with photocopies

alter the size of the source document by approximately 1% in either the horizontal or vertical direction.

Signatures written on digital tablets are not good exemplars for questioned signatures written with a pen or pencil. A few reasons are the signature on the digital tablet is not a continuous line, the tablets are often in awkward positions, and people often do not write a normal signature on the tablets. More details about writing on digital tablets is in Chapter 10.

Know the provenance of your data

Often document examiners rely upon the statements of the attorney on the origin of the exemplars. The attorney relies upon the client who supplies the exemplars. The true source of the exemplars used in the examination is unknown to the document examiner. A good practice is inclusion of a statement that an assumption of the examination is the known writing was written by the person stated as the source writer.

Most document examiners will not authenticate signatures of celebrities. The reason is there are many fraudulent and non-authentic celebrity signatures in circulation. There are many signatures, known as proxy signatures, signed by the celebrity's publicist or another authorized person. The document examiner may authenticate the signature yet the questioned signature and the exemplars may have been executed by the same person who is not the celebrity. This is also true of sports memorabilia. Many famous athletes authorize people to sign their name on a ball, shirt, or another item.

An example of where I was unintentionally misled as to the writer of an important exemplar is during the examination of a suspect in the famous Zodiac Killer case. The work was performed for the New York Times best-selling book *The Most Dangerous Animal of All* then later published in my book *The End of the Zodiac Mystery*. My client purported a marriage certificate was written by the suspect, his father, rather than the minister. His mother told him she had witnessed her husband write the entries on the marriage certificate. Later he learned his mother had not told him the truth. The minister had written the text on the marriage certificate. The misidentification of the author of the marriage certificate did not change my opinion that the person who wrote the marriage certificate probably wrote the Zodiac's letters. The identification of the writer changed.

A famous case from 1983 in which the source of the exemplars caused substantial international controversy was identification of the Hitler Diaries. Three internationally famous document examiners were retained to independently examine and opine on the authenticity of the diaries. Two identified the writer as Adolf Hitler. The third eliminated Hitler as the writer of the diaries. The third person was correct. The difference was the first two document examiners unknowingly compared the diaries with other forgeries written by the same person who wrote the diaries. The third person compared the diaries to Hitler's true writing. The exemplars provided to each document examiner were presented as authentic exemplars of Hitler's writing.

According to the SAFE and SWGDOC standards for handwriting identification, the document examiner must compare the exemplars to determine whether they were written by the same person. Once it is determined that the exemplars have been written by the same person, they can be used for comparison with the questioned writing.

Request exemplars

When an insufficient number of existing exemplars are available to perform an examination, the suspect may be asked to provide examples of their handwriting in front of the forensic document examiner. The writing may be a series of signatures, the text in question or text that represents words and characters in the questioned writing. The Scientific Association of Forensic Examiners (https://safeforensics.org) published a standard for taking request exemplars.

The writer should be placed in a setting that emulates the environment in which the questioned writing was likely written. Since the document examiner was not present when the questioned writing was written, the document examiner does not know for certain the environment in which the questioned writing was executed. The document examiner makes a best estimate on the environment. This reasoning must be stated in any written report. The document examiner should be present to observe the request writing. At the writing session, notes will be taken as to:

- the hand used for writing.
- the grip used to hold the writing instrument.
- the make and model of the writing instrument.
- posture of the writer.
- The speed at which the writing was executed.
- Pauses taken during the writing.

The document examiner presents the page on which the writing is to be made to the writer. The questioned writing is not shown to the writer. This prevents the writer from directly copying the questioned writing or intentionally disguising the writing so as not to resemble the questioned writing.

An exception to this rule is when the document examiner wants to learn how well a person is able to simulate a person's signature from a model of the signature. In this case, the subject may be asked to do their best to imitate the questioned signature. When this is done, the exercise should be conducted after the subject writes the questioned signature and or writing without seeing the questioned signature. The subject should not be told that the model is the questioned signature.

After a writing is executed, the document examiner removes the written page from the visibility of the writer. Another page is given to the writer. The writer writes the text again. If the writing is a signature, the same signature is again written. For a signature, the document examiner can present the writer with a duplicate of the page on which the questioned signature was written. The writing page is created by removing the questioned signature from the page. The signature location is used for the person to write the request exemplar. This procedure best simulates the environment in which the questioned signature was written.

The writer may be asked to write with the unaccustomed hand and the normal hand. This exercise determines whether the questioned writing may have been written by the suspect using the unaccustomed hand.

When text is to be written for request exemplars, the same type of paper on which the questioned writing is written should be used. If the questioned writing is on blank paper, blank paper is used for the request writing. If lined paper is used, lined paper with the same line density is used. The paper size is best if it is the same size as the paper on which the questioned writing is written. Lined paper should have the lines separated in the request page the same line separation as in the questioned document.

Examples of obtaining request exemplars
In criminal cases, I have gone to the jail to obtain request writing exemplars from the defendant. In one case, a question arose whether the defendant had written a letter to a person. Here I created four paragraphs containing the words in the questioned writing. Each paragraph used the words in a different order, yet provided enough words in the same order as the questioned writing to cause the writer to demonstrate desired attributes. Some of the attributes were letter spacing, word spacing, use of margins, formation of letters, and other attributes of the writing. Each paragraph was dictated to the writer three times for a total of 12 writing samples. The order of presentation of the paragraphs was mixed so the writer could not anticipate the next paragraph. The writing session was

conducted with the writer sitting in a chair at a table. I offered five pens to him. He selected the pen that he found most comfortable.

The text allegedly written by the defendant

10-24-07

Tomas,

I'm writing these few lines to let you know and anyone that is in doubt about mando. The vato is no foundation. He or his brother has no say so. Don't believe them when they use my name. If they have any questions you know how to get at me. Alright homie I hope this all gets right.

Con Respecto Tu,
Camarada
Pete

Text for one of the four request paragraphs

10-24-07

I'm writing a few lines about mando in the organization. The vato and his brother use my name to get people to doubt about the truth. Don't believe them when they say you know how to get at me. The vato has no foundation and his brother has no mando. Ask them if they have any questions for me about the disposable camera I use to entertain myself. Alright homie, I hope this all gets right. You know how I like to snap pictures of visual destinations.

Con respecto Tu,
Camarada
Pete

My opinion in this case was the defendant did not write the questioned document. There were unique attributes in his writing of the request exemplars and the many letters that he had written from jail that did not appear in the questioned writing. The deputy who monitors letters written by prisoners to people outside also said she did not recognize the writing in the questioned document as being that of defendant. The questioned document was excluded from trial because the US attorney had shredded the original.

In another criminal case, the defendant was accused of having signed his wife's name on many checks. Since he was in jail, the public defender asked his wife to come to their office for a request writing session. I presented her with 60 checks. She was asked to sign a blank check. I removed the check from her presence then presented her with another blank check. This method allowed me to see where she wrote on the check relative to the signature line, the hand used to write, the writing grip on the pen, the speed of writing and her posture. The speed at which the checks were presented was varied.

I could always observe the writer. Notes were taken on how the pen was held, the speed of execution, writing posture, and any other information of assistance in the investigation.

In this case, I opined that the defendant's wife had signed the checks in question. The case was dropped against the defendant and he was released from jail.

It is important for the attorney to work with the document examiner when request exemplars are required. The document examiner will provide guidance for taking the exemplars. Your case may be compromised if the request exemplars are taken incorrectly. Incorrect request exemplars may cause writing that is not representative of the needed writing samples.

Examples of not working with the document examiner
A question arose whether the defendant signed a traffic citation. To obtain writing exemplars for trial, the police asked the suspect to write his signature more than 30 times on the same page while sitting at a desk in a lighted room. The questioned signature was written late at night in a car on a dark road on a citation pad. The request exemplars differed from the questioned signature, and a qualified opinion was rendered. The police failed to engage a document examiner when taking the request exemplars.

In another case, I recommended to my retaining attorney that we demand request exemplars from the defendant in a civil case. The opposing side was uncooperative in providing enough examples of the defendant's writing. The attorney did not consult with me about what was needed for the request exemplars. He submitted a motion to the court to obtain the request exemplars from the defendant. The motion contained text of a paragraph the suspect would write.

The motion demanded that the defendant provide one example of his handwriting and one example of his signature. At the writing session, we obtained one sample from the suspect. The written text was of no value. The paragraph approved by the court contained long uncommon words that most people could not spell without pausing to consider possible spellings. We had one signature for comparison. In this example, the attorney needed to include a request for the suspect to sign and initial duplicate copies of the contract on which the questioned signatures and initials appeared.

Fortunately, there were other signatures the defendant had signed during negotiations with the plaintiff. A qualified opinion was reached that the suspect had written the questioned signature. The arbitrator ruled in favor of my attorney client's client. The key piece of evidence was discovered using a microscope to examine intricacies of the questioned signature and the known signatures. Figure 8.6 Disguised writing shows this microscopic image.

Chapter 7

Variability of handwriting

No two people write alike

A primary theory underlying handwriting comparison is that no two people write exactly the same. This theory is open to controversy. The list of potential writers must be limited to the list of people who potentially could have written the questioned document rather than the population of all people. There are more than 300 million people in the United States. It is nearly impossible to test the theory that no two people write in the same manner. How do we know that no two of the 300 million people write the same way?

When applying the theory that no two people write alike, the

Figure 7.1 Writing of two people

document examiner looks at the sample of potential writers of a document, then examines the likelihood two of the possible authors write alike. By reducing the sample size, the chances of finding two identical writers is reduced to minimal chances.

In the example in Figure 7.1, the writer of the exemplars wrote the bottom two signatures. The top writing of the word Tyler was written by the person who wrote a check to the writer of the exemplars. Notice how closely the writing styles are to each other. Since the writing of the top word Tyler was written as the name of the person to whom the check was made, there was no attempt at simulating Mrs. Tyler's name on this check. This is an example of why document examiners must be very careful in their comparison of attributes of signatures. Another difference between the top writing and the bottom two writings is the top writing was written using a signature line. The bottom two were written on unlined and paper.

The point is, some people write in a very similar manner. Both people probably learned the same writing style. The attributes of a common learned style are called class characteristics. ASTM Standard E1732-17 defines class characteristic: "The attributes that establish membership in a class."

Handwriting in the Latin-based alphabets is divided into three zones shown in Figure 7.2. The middle zone is the area in which most lower-case letters are written. These are letters such as a, e, r, s, etc. The upper zone is the area above the middle zone letters. The top of capital letters and some lower-case letters such as b, d, f, etc. extend into the upper zone. The lower zone is the area below the baseline or bottom of the middle zone letters. The bottom of lower-case letters, such as g, y, f, etc., extend into the lower zone.

SWGDOC Standard Terminology for Forensic Document Examiners, defines baseline as "the ruled or imaginary line upon

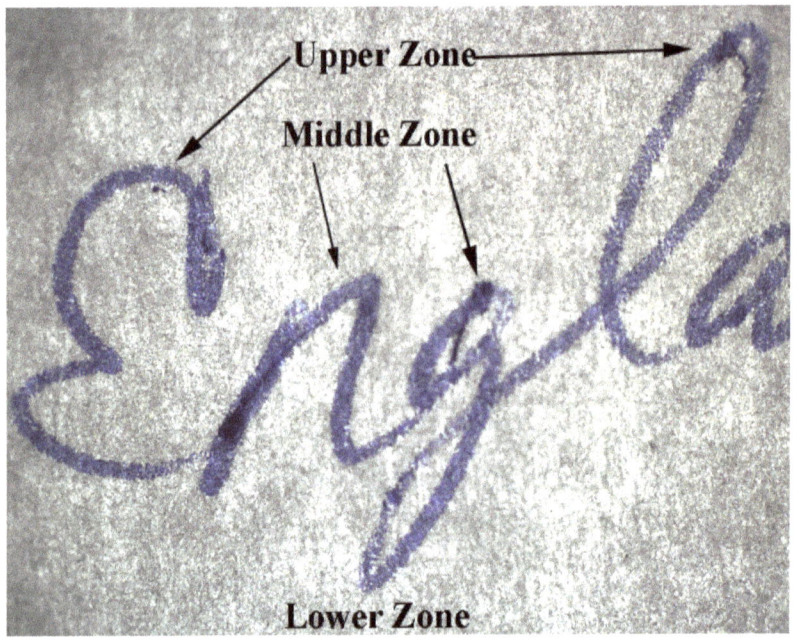

Figure 7.2 Writing Zones

which writing or typewriting appears to rest." This may differ from a signature line drawn on a page on which a person signs their name. A baseline may be horizontal. It may decline, rise, or oscillate.

Inter-writer variability is the way writing varies across different writers. In Figure 7.3 four writers construct the lower case cursive letter "y" in the word "quickly." All images were taken with a Mi-Scope digital microscope at 12x magnification. Although three of the writers use a stick formation for the lower zone, they are all written very differently. The upper left example slopes down to the right. The upper right is close to vertical. The lower left slopes down to the left. The examples on the left and bottom right are made with a single stroke, whereas the upper right example is constructed with two strokes. The lower right example places a loop in the lower zone on the loop at the bottom of the "y".

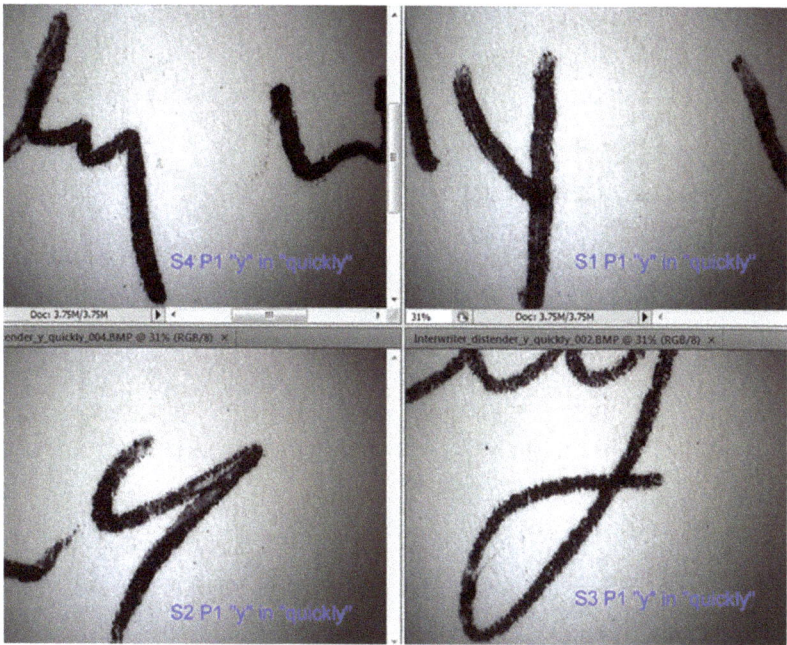

Figure 7.3 Inter-Writer Variability

NO PERSON WRITES EXACTLY THE SAME TWICE

A second theory of handwriting identification is that no two writings by the same person are ever exactly identical. The differences in the way a person writes among sessions is called intra-writer variability as shown in Figure 7.4. Only machines can create the same writing multiple times. Even writing by a machine has slight differences among writings. A document examiner looks at how a person writes because there is variability in the way each person writes. This variability must be defined to determine whether the questioned writing lies within the variability of the known writing.

Figure 7.4 shows that the distended portion of the "y" differs in each of these examples which were written by the same person in different words during two writing sessions. The examples on the top row were written on the same day with at least 15 minutes between writings to avoid exact replication of the writings. The

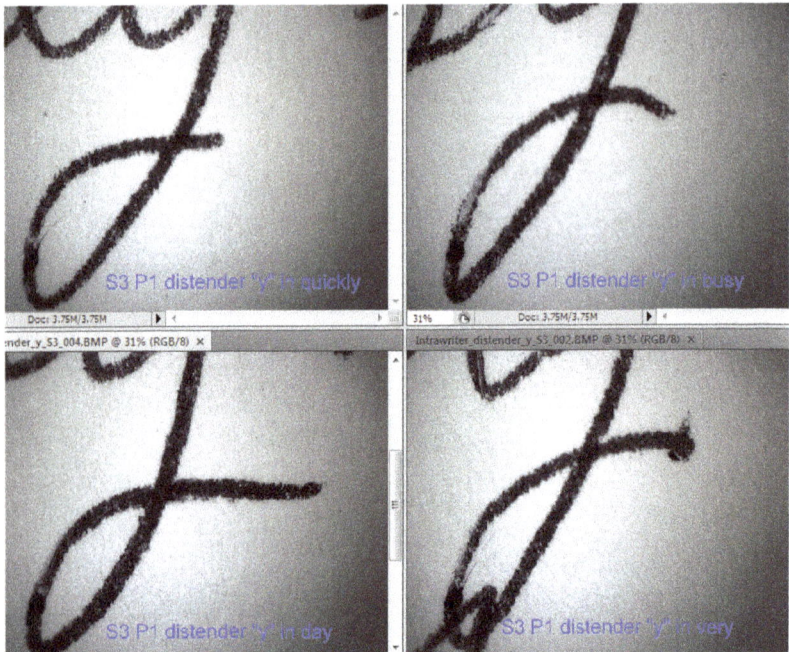

Figure 7.4 Intra-Writer Variability

bottom row was written on a day different from the top row writings. The same text was written for each writing session.

The upper left is the word quickly, the upper right is the word busy, the bottom left is the word day, and the lower right is the word very. Note that each example has an ink goop in the same location on the upstroke at the bottom of the "y". The upper left example has a wider loop than the other three. The terminus of the stroke in the upper left makes an up-stroke that does not exist in the other examples. The length of the horizontal terminal stroke in the upper right is longer than the other three examples. The terminal stroke in the bottom left image does not cross the down stroke of the "y".

Variability of handwriting is demonstrated in the changes in formation of characteristics of writing from session to session. Although

the overall attributes of writing are similar across writing sessions, the attributes will differ slightly each time a word is written.
Examples of variability (not all inclusive) are:
- the height of a letter.
- the width of a letter.
- The height to width ratio of the letter.
- The ratio of the height of two letters
- the width of a word.
- the angle of a stroke.
- the elevation of a word relative to a signature line.
- placement of an i-dot.
- pressure of the pen on the page.

Calculating the height to width ratio of a letter is valuable as a quantitative measure of handwriting. Use of ratios is presented in detail later in this chapter.

The document examiner determines the extent of variability in the known writing. Some writing is very consistent across sessions. Other people's writing shows a wide range of variability. Consistent writing offers a better opportunity for the document examiner to determine whether the questioned writing fits the pattern of the known writing. When the known writing shows much variability, the document examiner often must look for more intricate consistent attributes of the known writing. This often requires enlargement of the writing using a microscope or computer software such as Photoshop.

Ordway Hilton wrote, "Habits may be retained that persist across natural evolution of a signature during a person's lifetime. (Hilton, 1992)" Figure 7.5 includes samples of my writing from 1979 through 2009. One item to notice is the little mark, or goop, in the upstroke of the lower loop of lower-case letters. This goop always appears, regardless of writing instrument or posture used when writing.

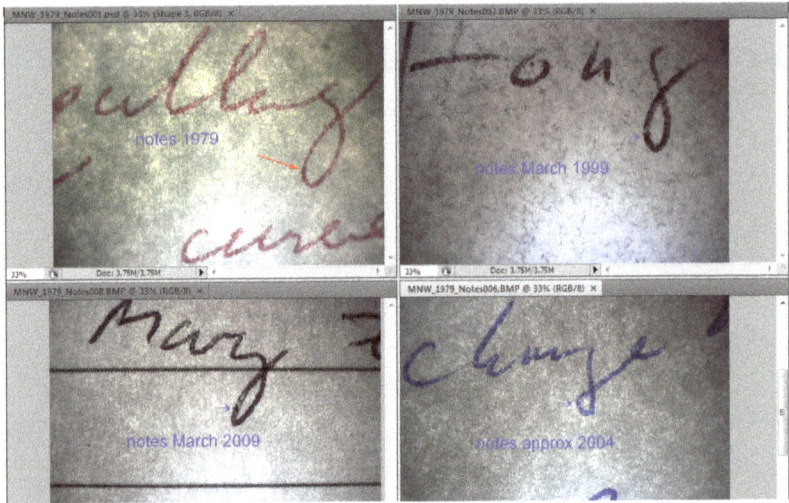

Figure 7.5 Writing habits

A goop at this location in a writing does not indicate the writing is mine as other people place a goop at this location in the writing. The writer of the words in Figure 7.4 also placed goop in a similar location on the loop of the lower zone letter. What the goop indicates is that if I were a suspect, a clue has been found. This clue tells the document examiner to continue looking for clues in the questioned writing that are common in the known writing. Writer identification is a result of discovery of many clues in the known writing that are also common in the questioned writing without any consistent significant differences between the known and questioned writings. The small attributes in the writing are difficult for the simulator to copy. Large attributes can be traced or copied by a skilled artist.

A basic theory of handwriting is there is a consistency in a person's writing. A person is incapable of changing these attributes of writing. Writing is a habit. As we develop graphic maturity, we develop habits that identify the writing as ours regardless of writing instrument used. These anomalies can be another clue to identify the writer. Because writing is a habit, it is not just the big structures we make in a similar manner, but we also make the microstructures in a similar manner. These goops result from neuro-muscular interaction a person cannot control.

Robert Saudek (Saudek, 1929) identified "blobs" in writing as caused by the writer. Saudek wrote, "Frequent pauses during writing, recognizable by meaningless blobs, blobs due to readjustment, angles, divided letters and unrhymical separations within the word itself, . . . and touching up of letters.

TYPES OF VARIATION
Common cause variation
Common cause variation, also called natural variation, is the variability in writing that happens from writing session to writing session. This intra-writer variability is explainable. Common cause variability in handwriting results from occurrences such as change of posture, different writing instrument, fatigue of the writer, the purpose of the writing, aging of the writer, illness, etc.

Variation occurs because a person's muscles do not move in exactly the same manner for each writing session, even when there are no confounding events.

Special cause variation
Special cause variation is any factor that can be detected and identified as contributing to a change in a person's writing. This is not explainable or attributable to the writer. Examples may be a rough line caused by a rough writing surface or a sudden jump caused when the writer was startled. When these appear in the known writing, the examples are disregarded for the analysis. An unexplained anomaly in a questioned writing may result from special cause variability.

USE OF STATISTICAL TECHNIQUES

When applying the scientific method, the common cause (natural) variability can be measured mathematically and shown on a plot. This reduces subjective bias from the analysis. The numbers do not lie or mislead. The document examiner uses the charts to determine whether the ratio of the questioned writing lies within the ratios of the expected common cause variability of the known writing. These charts are called control charts.

An indication the writer of the known writing also wrote the questioned writing occurs when the ratio of the questioned writing lies within the common cause variability of the known writing. A good simulation of the known writing may also lie within the expected common cause variability. Therefore, when the questioned writing lies within the common cause variability of the known writing, the document examiner continues the examination to discover whether other corroborating evidence of the same or different writers exists.

Application of mathematical variability was independently described in 1929 by both Osborn and Saudek. Osborn described the consistency to the height to the length of a word across writing sessions. Saudek wrote, "... the relative sizes of the different categories of letters ... are therefore bound up with his writing movement in a particularly persistent fashion ... (p 204)" On page 142 of Questioned Documents, Osborn wrote, "Genuine writing or genuine signatures show a certain definite and fixed proportion of height of letters to length of words." The necessary statistical techniques had not been developed at the time of their writings. Osborn did not show the method used to arrive at this conclusion.

Applying statistical techniques, Jindal, et. al. (1999) refuted Osborn's statement. They showed that the ratio of the height to length of a signature is not an appropriate indicator of a writer.

As stated by Saudek, comparing the physical height of a letter in a word or signature to the physical height of the same letter in another word or signature is not important for comparison. The height will vary due to the space offered for writing the word or signature. Some pages offer constrained spaces such as boxes or writing lines. Other pages are blank with no constraints on the size of the writing.

The important aspect is the ratio of the letters to each other. As an example, if the letters "he" appear in the words, the ratio of the height of the "h" to the "e" is calculated in each word of the known writing. The ratio of the "h" to "e" is calculated in the questioned writing. The ratio is compared statistically to the ratio in the known writing to learn whether the questioned writing lies within the common cause (natural) variability of the known writing.

Measure ratios of letters

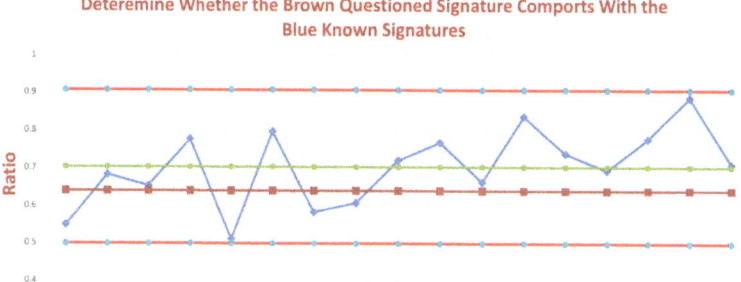

Figure 7.6 Control chart of the natural variation of ratios

The chart in Figure 7.6 determines whether the questioned writing falls within range of the way the known writer writes, or intra-writer variability. Brugnatelli (2013) expanded on the observations of Saudek. He reported the results of comparing the height of letters. He discovered the height of capital letters is not a good indicator of writer identification. Letters internal to the word are the best indicators. Brugnatelli showed statistical confirmation that the ratio of letters is a valid indicator for identification of a writer. It is only one indicator, not conclusive evidence.

Other statistical tests are conducted to determine the quality of the data, whether the data is sufficient, etc. These tests are outside the scope of this book.

In July, 2015, I delivered a presentation titled, "Using statistical analysis to assist with writer identification" at the International Symposium on Forensic Science Error Management in Arlington, VA. The symposium was sponsored by the National Institute for Standards and Technology.

The chart in Figure 7.6 represents the results of measuring the ratio of the height of the upper zone divided by the height of the middle zone. The height of the upper zone is determined by measuring the height of the tallest letter in the signature. The height of the middle zone is determined by measuring the height of the tallest letter in the middle zone. The height of the upper zone is divided by the height of the middle zone to obtain the ratio or proportion as stated in criterion 21 of Huber and Hedrick's 21 criteria.

The wavy blue line represents the ratio of the upper zone height for the letter h to the middle zone height for the letter o in Jonathan for each known signature. This shows the ratio varies for each known signature. This is the intra-writer variability of the known writer. It is the way the writer changes the relative heights of the upper zone and middle zone of his name each time they write.

The straight line with the squares represents the ratio of the upper zone h to the middle zone ratio o in the questioned writing. The chart shows the ratio in the signature of the questioned writing lies within the natural variation of the ratios of the known writing. Therefore, the document examiner has empirical evidence the writer of the questioned writing may be the writer of the known writing.

This is one piece of evidence. It does not mean the writer of the known writing is the writer of the questioned writing. A good simulator may be able to write a signature that falls within the statistical attributes of the known writing. A traced signature will lie within the expected variability of the known writing.

To apply this test, the document examiner takes several measurements of the known and questioned writing. These measurements may include the angle of writing or spacing between words. These measurements add to the evidence. The height ratios of several letter permutations are compared. The reason for permutations rather than combinations is the order sequence in which the letters are written is important. People often write the same letter in different forms depending on the location of the letter in the word. An example of the same combination is abc, bca, cba. These are different permutations of the same letters.

Although the attributes of one measurement of the questioned writing may align with the known writing, it is unlikely the attributes of several measurements will align with the known writing when the writing is simulated.

It is possible that even though the person appears to have written the questioned signature, another person may have similar variability in their writing.

Measure angles of the writing

Document examiners must determine the cause of the difference between the writings to determine whether a person wrote a document or signature. They must understand possible illusions in writing caused by extraneous marks on a page, such as machine printed writing, drawings, color of paper or other distractions that may cause a writing to look different from another when it may have the same attributes.

In Figure 7.7, the line that moves up and down represents the measurements of the angle of the "N" in the known writing. The

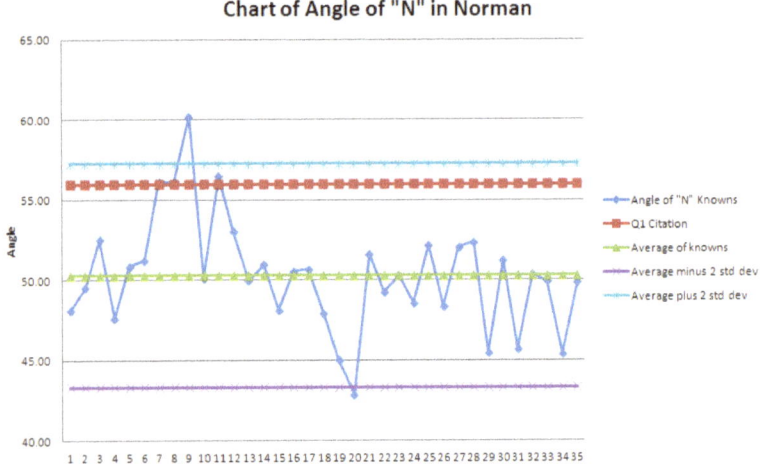

Figure 7.7 Natural Variation of the Angle of Writing

line shows the intra-writer variation. Each number at the bottom of the chart represents a known writing sample. There were 35 known signatures. The dot at the angle represents the angle of a stroke in the relevant stroke in the word "Norman." For known sample 1, the angle was approximately 47 degrees. The angle for sample 2 was approximately 48 degrees. The angle for sample 3 was approximately 52 degrees. The horizontal line toward the top with the square box markers represents the angle for the "N" in the word "Norman" in the questioned document. The line in the center shows the average of the angles for the known writing samples.

In this example, the questioned writing falls within a statistically defined intra-writer variability. Therefore, the writer is a valid suspect for having written the questioned writing. The implication is we must continue with the examination using other generally accepted methods for handwriting identification. A scientific approach is used in this example which demonstrates criterion 6 of Huber and Hedrick's 21 criteria.

Application of measurement and mathematics to writer identification is not new. The ASTM/SWGDOC standards encourage knowledge of mathematics for the forensic document examiner. ASTM/SWGDOC standard E444, *Standard Guide for the Scope of Work of Forensic Document Examiners*, states that education from fields such as ". . . physical sciences, mathematics . . ." are important for the forensic document examiner.

In 1914, Frank Freeman wrote about measurement of speed and angles of writing. Freeman stated on page 144, "we have not yet sufficient data for complete application of these principles to writing." In 1929, Robert Saudek expanded on Freeman's work when he published measurement results in *Experiments With Handwriting*. Later, Albert Osborn, Wilson Harrison, Ordway Hilton and others wrote about application of proportion of writing zones to assist identification of a writer. Huber and Hedrick applied the concept of the likelihood ratio to writer identification.

Chapter 8

Authentication of handwriting

This chapter offers detailed information about handwriting identification. The purpose is to offer the reader insights into how forensic handwriting examination is performed. The intent is not to make the legal professional a forensic handwriting examiner. The intent is to provide the legal professional reading this book enough insight to properly vet a prospective forensic handwriting examiner.

Document examiners have very different training backgrounds and they vary significantly in experience level and expertise. Since no licensing is required in this profession, you will find that who you select as your expert can affect the opinion you receive, and therefore determine the outcome of your case.

Because this is true, and because you must determine when document examination can help you with your case, it is advisable that you have a strong grasp of what can be determined through this science.

This information provides a good basis to understand basic handwriting examination techniques, tools, procedures, and the basis of opinions.

Photoshop is a powerful tool that enables the document examiner to extract desired sections of a document, such as a signature, and remove all undesired background markings. Background markings can subconsciously induce false perceptions of the writing or other parts of the document. This procedure facilitates an unbiased comparative analysis.

SIMULATION OF WRITING

Document examiners do not use the word "forge" since forgery implies intent and mental condition. Forgery is a legal term for a trier of fact to determine. A document examiner opines only that a document is genuine or not genuine.

The term "simulation" indicates that another person copied or traced someone's known signature or writing. The "simulator" is the person who does the copying or tracing.

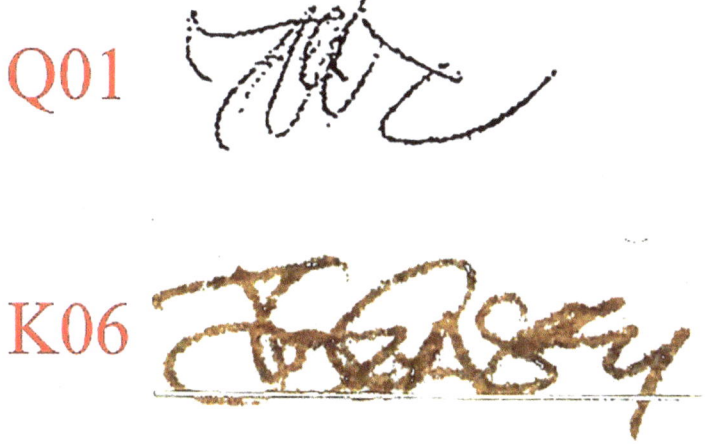

Figure 8.1 Freehand Simulation

Freehand simulation, Figure 8.1, occurs when a person does not try to create an exact copy of the other person's writing.

This may be done when:

1. The simulator believes the recipient of the writing is not familiar with the writing style of the person whose writing is being simulated.
2. The recipient will not verify the writing.
3. The person whose writing has been simulated will not see the document containing the simulated writing.

In Figure 8.1 the questioned signature (Q01) was written on a newly inserted page of a contract signed by the known writer (K06). Standard nomenclature is using the letter Q to indicate the questioned writing, and the letter K to indicate the known writing. Apparently, the person who added this page to the contact believed the true signer would not notice the new terms it included.

When a document examiner must determine whether a specific person simulated a signature, the examiner should obtain the regular writing of the suspect, and sample signatures.

When a person simulates someone else's signature, the result is not a signature. It is drawing a signature. A simulated signature may be similar in form and appearance to the simulator's regular course-of-business writing. Course of business writing is that which appears on business correspondence, checks, contracts, and other writing performed in business settings.

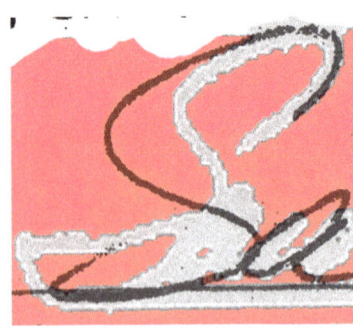

Figure 8.2 Simulation

In a different case involving a simulated signature (Figure 8.2), I had examples of both the suspected simulator's signature and regular writing. The simulator and the person whose name was simulated shared the letter "S" as the first letter of their first names.

When I compared the simulator's actual signature with the signature he simulated, the first letters of the name in his signature and the questioned signature did not match.

When I extracted the letter S from the simulator's course of business writing and compared it with the first letter of the simulated signature, they were very similar.

The name of the person whose signature was on the questioned document was Simon, seen in the white letter on the red background. I compared the "S" in Simon with the S in the word "Same," shown in black from the known writing of the suspect.

Figure 8.3 Simulation

I sized the images proportionally so the height of the known and questioned writings was approximately the same. The shape of the letter S was within expected normal variability of the known writer. The angles comported with each other.

Figure 8.3 shows another case in which a person simulated the name "Stella". Her "St" from normal course-of-business writing matched the "St" in the simulated the name "Stella".

The red writing is the questioned writing. The black writing is the simulator's known writing. When I placed the questioned writing on top of the known writing, although there are differences, the similarities were apparent. There were many other strong similarities between the questioned and known writings. There were no significant differences repeated between the known and questioned writings.

Figure 8.3 is one of several comparisons that lead to an opinion of, "strong probability wrote." This is one of the nine standard opinions offered by forensic document examiners as defined in SAFE and SWGDOC standards. The standards state this opinion means the document examiner "virtually certain" the questioned writing was written by the known writer.

In each case of simulation, the person was unable to change their standard writing style when attempting to simulate a signature. This was true even when the person's first initial was the same as the first initial of the name he simulated.

Since a simulated signature is a drawing of a signature rather than a true signature, the result is that the simulated signature is a variation of the writer's everyday writing.

WRITING DIRECTION AS A DIFFERENTIATOR

Authorities in document examination state that people write in a specific manner to construct strokes. For instance, they move in a clockwise or counterclockwise direction each time the same letter is formed. This is an unconscious motion. The person's brain instructs the muscles to move is a specific direction, either clockwise or counterclockwise.

Figure 8.4 Writing direction

In Figure 8.4 the person who wrote the name "Margaret" wrote the letter "a" twice in the same word. Upon initial examination, in the first instance the lower loop is written counterclockwise. In the second instance, the lower loop appeared to have been written in a clockwise direction.

A closer examination was performed by using Photoshop to enlarge the image. The exposure tool was used to enhance the image.

The examination revealed the second "a" is constructed like the first "a." The loop is made in a counterclockwise direction.

I examined the second "a" in Margaret with NEGA software in Figure 8.5. This software is used to determine line sequence. The purpose is to determine whether the down stroke comes to a point then continues up to the left or whether it continues around in a counterclockwise direction terminating at the intersection of the two lines.

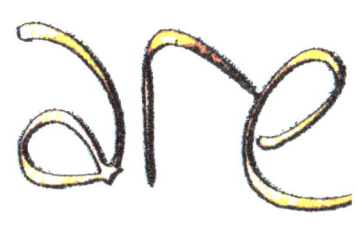

Figure 8.5 NEGA software for writing direction

The examination revealed that the down stroke stops at the point then moves upward to the left in a counterclockwise direction. Application of magnifying the writing and using the enhancement techniques of the NEGA software reveals the truth about the writing. Examination with the naked eye gave an allusion this letter "a" had been written in a clockwise direction.

NEGA software is created by a Spanish software company, MacWinlin.

Disguised writing

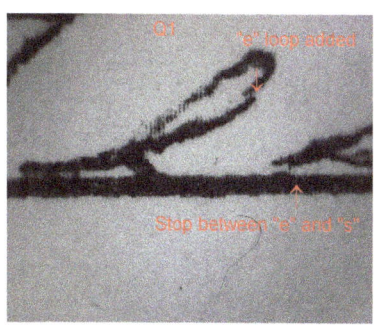

Figure 8.6 Disguised writing

Disguised writing is also known as auto-simulation or auto forgery. A person intentionally disguises a signature or other writing with the intention of disavowing execution of the writing. The purpose may be to later deny having signed a contract or another type of document.

In one case, a person denied having executed a real estate contract. With the naked eye, his signature appeared generally fluid.

In his known writing, the writer always stopped writing after the "e", leaving a gap before starting the next letter in his name: "s". When examined under the microscope at 40 times (40x) magnification, in Figure 8.6, the gap is apparent in the questioned signature.

However, in the known exemplars, the lower case "e" was always written as a single, retraced stroke (appearing more like a forward-slanted, undotted "i").

When I examined the signature in Figure 8.6, it was apparent that a patch stroke had been added to the top to disguise the letter e, making it look more like a regular "e".

In this questioned signature, the writer apparently attempted to disguise the letter "e". This attempt failed when the strokes were magnified.

The arbitrator agreed with my results and my attorney client prevailed.

In another case, I opined the signature was probably disguised. The signature was a stylized signature. A stylized signature is a signature which the writer scrawls their name so the letters are not identifiable.

Many attributes of the signature bore strong similarities to the known signature of the writer. Due to the complexity and intricate details of the signature, a simulator would have difficulty replicating the small details of the writer's known signature. Yet, there were substantial differences between the questioned signature and the 34 known signatures.

In deposition, the person admitted having signed the document after imbibing alcoholic beverages.

The lesson learned is not all signatures that appear disguised are disguised. The plaintiff originally denied having signed the document. I cannot know whether she disguised the signature to later disavow it or whether the differences resulted from the alcohol.

INFIRMITY

Figure 8.7 Infirm person's writing

The document examiner must learn whether the writer of the known documents has an illness or other infirmity which may have affected the writing.

Diseases of the central nervous system, muscles, pulmonary system, or cardiovascular system can induce changes in writing. When infirmity is present, the document examiner will request writing exemplars from the time of the questioned writing to show writing that either includes or excludes the infirmity.

If the person is infirm, the analysis may be more complex than when the person has no infirmity. The example in Figure 8.7 shows the tremor induced by illness in an elderly person. This is a known signature from the person whose writing was compared with a questioned signature.

Here, the questioned signature showed little tremor and better speed. Therefore, the questioned signature, which was written at approximately the same time as the known signatures, was a better-quality writing than the person was capable of executing. It is also possible that the writer had been taking tremor reduction drugs which cause the writing to show less tremor.

The document examiner must learn whether the person used drugs to reduce the tremor before opining the difference is due to two writers. In this case, Mary was not taking tremor reduction drugs.

Figure 8.8 shows the handwriting of an elderly man found in his house dehydrated. He was taken to the hospital where he recovered for a week.

The known exemplars were examined at the hospital. Although his writing improved daily, there was still substantial tremor in the

Figure 8.8 Infirm and Drug Side Effects

writing. Exemplars written prior to the dehydration incident showed tremor.

I requested to see the decedent's medical records to learn the source of the tremor in the writing. Tremor was listed as a side effects of a drug he was using. His tremor may have been induced by the drug. The document examiner's job is to discover the root cause of otherwise unexplained anomalies in writing. We learn whether what appears to be special cause variation is truly common cause variability. There are times the root cause cannot be known.

As a person ages or becomes infirm, there are often changes to the writing. We must ask questions. There have been cases where a person has tremulous writing at one time and smooth writing shortly thereafter due to drugs which quell the cause of tremor. Other changes may be due to injury.

In one case, I asked the attorney why there was a change in a person's signature after a given date. The person had injured his writing arm. It was necessary for me to ask whether the subject was taking medication to quell any tremor before rejecting the exemplars as being legitimate.

VERIFICATION OF EXEMPLARS – REFER TO STANDARD

A question may arise as to the authenticity of exemplars. Figure 8.9 is a situation where an attorney gave me a signature on a hospital intake form as an exemplar (image on right).

The letter "A" in this exemplar differed from those in all other exemplars for the subject. It was in the form of a printed "A". The "A" was cursive form in all the other exemplars (image on left) which spanned 50 years.

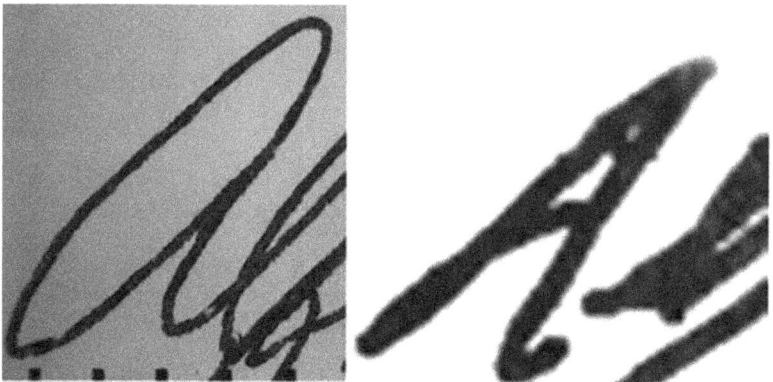

Figure 8.9 Variation of valid signatures

I questioned the authenticity of the exemplar. At my request, the attorney told his client additional exemplars of this format were needed for this to be accepted as an authentic exemplar.

Another similar print-style exemplar was produced. The additional exemplar was stipulated as authentic by the party on the other side of the case.

Therefore, I accepted the exemplar as demonstrating the subject had two distinct methods of writing the first letter of his name. Note that the forward slant and width of the "A" in both forms is similar.

The document examiner has a duty to question the authenticity of any exemplar that shows a significant difference from the other exemplars.

Document examiners can work with writing not in their native language. I met an Indian document examiner in China at the World Congress of Forensics. She asked me to assist with a case written in Hindi shown in Figure 8.10.

Although I cannot read Hindi, I discerned anomalies between the known writing (identified with the letter "A") and the questioned writing (identified with the letter "D"). Here, I used Photoshop to place the known and questioned signatures onto the same page for ease of comparison and exhibition.

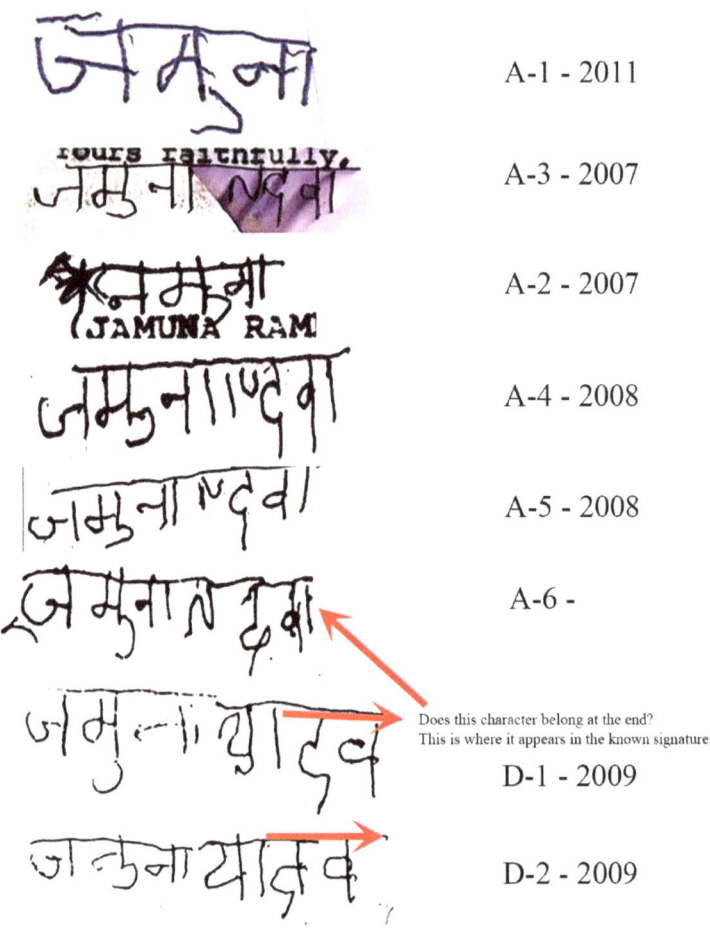

Figure 8.10 Hindi Writing

I have successfully examined Chinese signatures for authentication. The methodology used for comparison was to identify common attributes in the written symbols. I examined the stroke structure. Based on these attributes, I could successfully compare the questioned signature with the known signatures. My client identified the symbols that represented the questioned signatures and known signatures.

When examining Latin-based language other than the examiner's native language, or language in which the examiner is fluent, it is important to learn the class characteristics of the writing style. Class characteristics refer to the way you learned to write, or the writing system you were taught.

Recently I worked on an anonymous letter case in which the words were written in Polish. There were interesting common characteristics between the known and questioned writings. Upon researching the class characteristics of Polish writing, I learned that the letter construction was the result of a class characteristic, not an individual characteristic of the known writer. Class characteristics are the characteristics of the writing style learned by groups of people. Therefore, I eliminated these similarities as discriminators for potential identification of the known writer.

Robosigning

With robosigning, one person's name is on perhaps hundreds or thousands of documents, yet the documents were signed by many people who simulated the name.

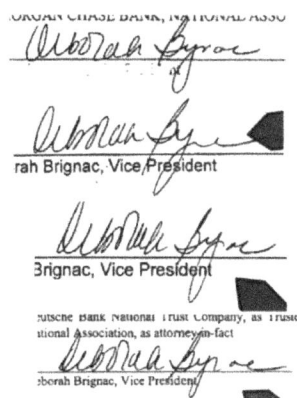

Figure 8.11 Robosigning

We do not know whether the documents were signed by the person whose signature appears on the signature line. A common usage of robosigning is with mortgage loan documents.

In the case shown in Figure 8.11, my client presented 11 certified copies of deeds from the county recorder's office. The documents had allegedly been signed by the same person. Although all the names were the same, many signatures varied significantly from each other. The client wanted to know whether more than one person had executed the signatures.

After reviewing each signature, it was apparent that many had been executed by different people. The signatures were followed by "/s," or initials indicating another person had signed the name. After removing those signatures from the set, the four documents shown in Figure 8.11 remained.

Examination of these four signatures indicated they were all signed by the same person. Since known signatures of this person were not available, there was no way to know whether these four signatures were true signatures of the person whose name is signed.

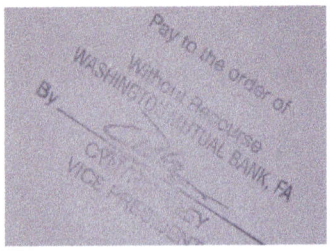

Figure 8.12 Rubber Stamp

Other examples of robosigning are performed with a rubber stamp or acrylic stamp. Figure 8.12 shows an example of a document where the signature was affixed using a stamp containing a signature. A pen was not used to sign the document.

COMPARE SIGNATURES USING PHOTOSHOP

Photoshop is used to compare signatures and other writing between a questioned document and known documents.

In Figure 8.13, the known signature is black and the questioned signature is red. The known signature was placed over the questioned signature to determine how well they comport with each other. We can see angles and stroke structure are similar.

Figure 8.13 Signature comparison match

Photoshop is also valuable for creating demonstrative exhibits for court. The exhibit in Figure 8.14 shows the difference between two questioned

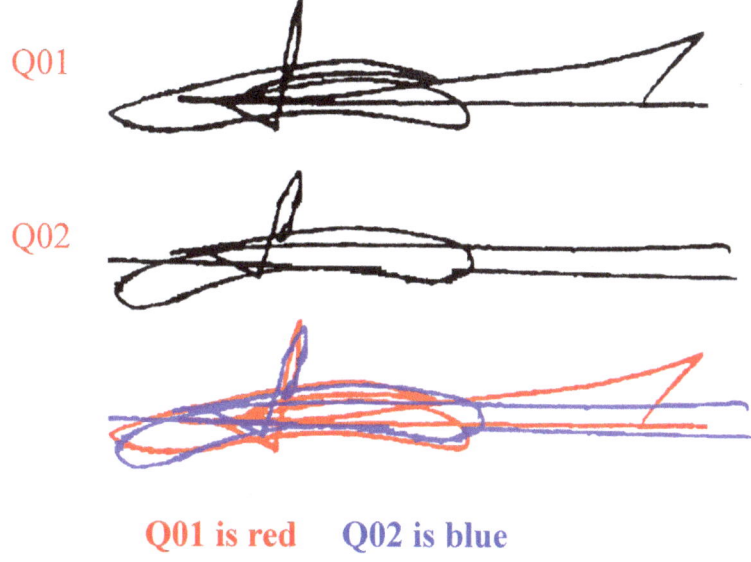

Figure 8.14 Compare two questioned signatures

signatures in a case. These signatures were on two documents in question. The signatures were superimposed on top of each other to determine whether they may have been authored by the same person. Since both signatures were provided as black photocopies, the color of each was changed for ease in distinguishing the superimposed signatures. This provides simple talking points for the document examiner in court.

Chapter 9

Altered documents

USING INFRARED LIGHT TO DISCOVER INK ALTERATIONS

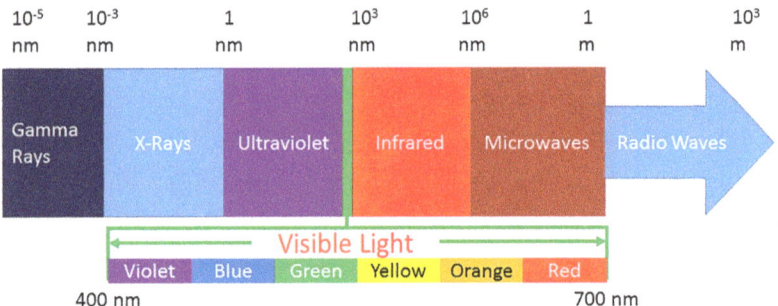

Figure 9.1 Electromagnetic Spectrum

Figure 9.1 shows the portion of the electromagnetic spectrum visible to the human eye. According to NASA (https://science-edu.larc.nasa.gov/EDDOCS/Wavelengths_for_Colors.html) visible light for humans is approximately from 400 nanometers (nm) to 700 nm. We see only a small portion of the electromagnetic spectrum.

Infrared light is the portion just above that which our eyes can see (from approximately 700 nm to 1000 nm). This light is visible to some animals and instruments that have been developed by humans.

The bottom of visible light appears violet, or purple to our eyes. The top appears red. Different objects appear as different colors to our eyes based on the frequency of light they reflect and absorb. Blue water has a different frequency than a green tree.

Filters with different infrared frequencies are used to examine writing. Some objects appear in some frequencies and not others. For example, an ink which is visible to your eyes may not be visible in certain infrared frequencies. When two lines are made using different inks, both may be visible to your eyes, but only one might be visible through an infrared filter.

White Light

Infrared 850 nanometers

Figure 9.2 Infrared light

This method is used for discriminating inks.

Devices such as the Video Spectral Comparator® (VSC) and HSI Examiner® allow the operator to set different frequencies of infrared and ultraviolet light. An examiner using a camera places different filters in front of the camera's lens to view the document using different frequencies.

Different inks reflect and absorb different portions of the electromagnetic spectrum. The filters permit only the desired frequency of light to pass through the filter. This is the same as placing a blue filter in front of your eye. Everything appears blue.

Similarly, objects may appear a similar color when viewed in visible light yet appear different when viewed in infrared light.

Figure 9.2 shows a clear example of how infrared light can be used to identify an alteration in writing where two inks were used.

In this example, the contract stated that a person owed $100 (bottom of Figure 9.2). However, the person owed the money added a line at the top of the 1, making it appear that the person owes $700 (top of Figure 9.2). Both portions of the seven were drawn in black ink.

The eye may not discern the alteration when viewed in white (visible) light. A document examiner has several tools which allow differentiation of the inks.

In the bottom example, the seven was examined under infrared light at frequency of 850 nanometers frequency. The infrared clearly shows two inks were used to construct the seven. The horizontal line virtually disappears under infrared light.

Figure 9.3 shows a portion of a holographic will photographed in white light. A question arose whether the decedent had written the will. The color of the words "after I die" appear similar to the remainder of the text.

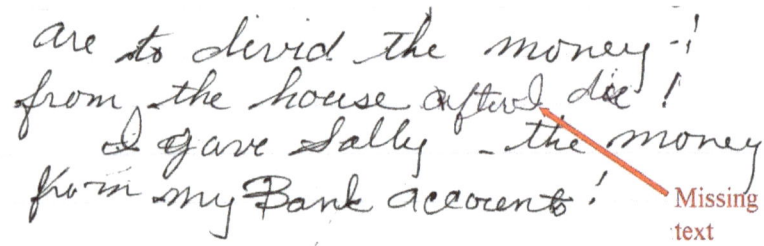

Figure 9.3 Image in white light

Other sections of the document were imaged in both white light and infrared light.

I configured a Nikon D70 camera to take photographs using infrared light. In Figure 9.4, I placed a filter on the lens allowing only infrared light to pass onto the photoreceptors in the camera.

The arrow points to a location on the document where the words "after I die" were written in black ink as seen in Figure 9.3. Although

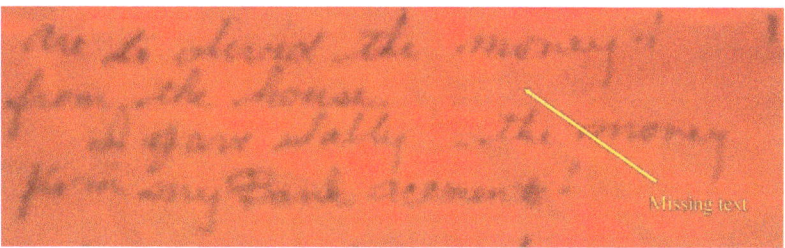

Figure 9.4 Image in infrared light

the entire document was written in black ink, infrared examination shows the words were added with a different pen subsequent to the writing of the rest of the document.

Examination of the document using various frequencies of infrared light demonstrated that at least four pens were used to write the document. For some underlined words, the underlines were made using two pens. Infrared light proved that different inks were used, revealing that the document was altered.

CUT AND PASTE ALTERATIONS

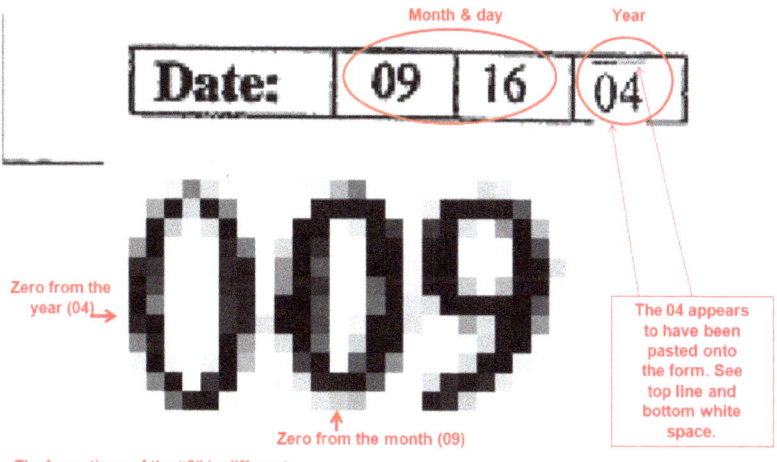

Figure 9.5 Altered document

Document examiners also examine documents produced using computer printers or other mechanical devices. Alterations can be revealed using many investigative methods.

In Figure 9.5, the year in the date was changed.

Several aspects indicate this alteration. Notice there is an extra line above the 04 that does not line up with the original box around the year. The line in the box below the 04 is missing. When the image is magnified, the zeros in the month and year do not match.

Different methods can create alterations like these:

> *Alteration method 1*: The year, "04", could have been printed on a separate piece of paper, then cut out and pasted on the original document. The paper with the "04" was oversized, and therefore, covered the line below the date. The extra line at the top could be a shadow created by the copier.

The differences in the zeros may be the result of using a second printer to print the "04", or using a different font from the same printer.

> *Alteration method 2*: The original document could have been electronically scanned. The "04" could have been created electronically in another document, then copied and placed onto the scanned image of the page. The "04" was not placed properly on the digital page.

Images on a computer are made of pixels (picture elements). The pixels are small dots which blend to give the appearance of a solid image to the naked eye.

When the characters are enlarged, the pixel formation of the number zero in the month differs from the pixel formation in the year. This shows they were printed using different printers or different fonts. In this example, I used Photoshop to enlarge the image to reveal the pixel construction.

Manual cut and paste alterations

Cut and paste is performed by cutting a known signature or other writing from a document, manually placing it on another document, and then making a copy of the manufactured document. When submitted, the copy is claimed to be a photocopy of the original document.

The photocopy may be scanned, then printed from the computer. The person who submits the document may claim they printed the document from a word processor such as Microsoft Word.

Since no person writes exactly the same twice, when two signatures are an exact match, the document examiner can be certain one is a cut and paste copy of the other. This can be detected when one signature is superimposed onto another signature using Photoshop or another software product such as PHOTO-PAINT®.

If both signatures appear on copies and not original documents, they may both be cut and paste copies of a third signature.

Using computer software such as Adobe Photoshop, cut and paste documents appear realistic on the computer screen. They may also be passed off as copies of legitimate documents.

When only copies are available, there may be no certain means to determine whether a document is authentic. The signature may be authentic yet could have been superimposed on the document by cut-and-paste techniques. There are instances where person creating the cut-and-paste leaves traces behind that expose the deed. These traces may be visible even when there is no source document available to the document examiner.

For this reason, always ask your client to provide the first-generation source document whenever it is available. If the document contains handwriting, request the document with the ink or pencil writing rather than a first generation copy or a scan of the source document. The original can be examined to determine whether the handwriting is authentic or fabricated.

Oftentimes, document examiners receive only photocopies of documents. This is especially true for exemplars. Many times, documents such as bank checks and copies of receipts are presented to the document examiner. This is the case because in many instances the original document is retained by the merchant or party that presented a contract for signature. In these instances, the buyer is given a photocopy of the original document. In many instances with contracts the buyer is given a backup copy of a no carbon required (NCR) set of pages. The NCR form is a set of identical pages on which writing is performed on the top page. Small ink bubbles in the subsequent pages burst from the pressure of pen as writing is executed. This transfer is an image of the signature on to the lower pages.

In Figure 9.6, for illustration, using Adobe Photoshop I copied and pasted the signature and date from the tax form onto the signature line of the check .

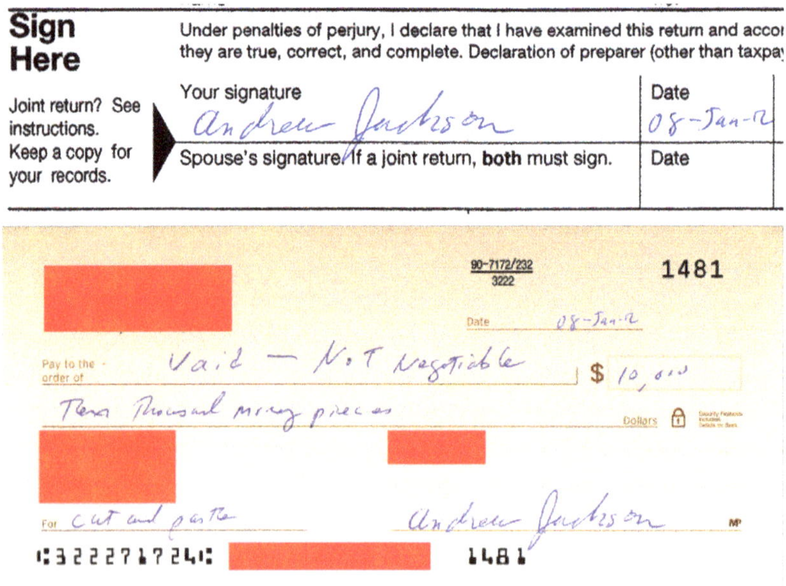

Figure 9.6 Cut and paste

The question is, which signature is real, or were both signatures cut and pasted from a third document? Unless the original document is examined, the document examiner may not be able to determine whether one is a scan of an original.

To properly identify if writing has been cut and pasted, both signatures must be extracted and placed one on top of the other using Photoshop or another technique. If there is an exact match, one is a copy of the other or both are a copy of a third signature.

Figure 9.7 Cut and paste overlay

In Figure 9.7, the signature of Andrew Jackson from the tax form was placed over the signature on the check. The example shows a slight offset to differentiate the two signatures, which fit exactly over each other.

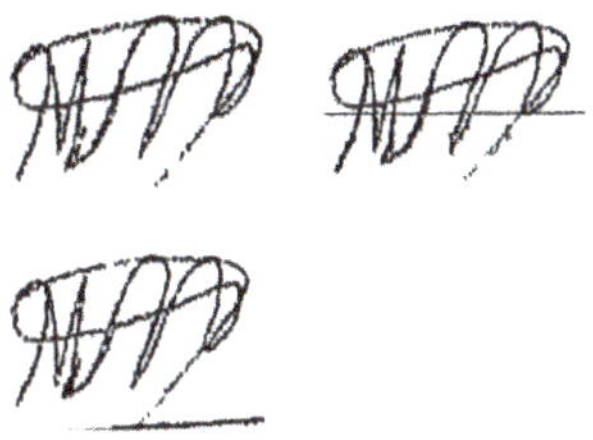

Figure 9.8 shows an example where the plaintiff stated he did not sign several documents.

Each of the three signatures came from a different document. Examination revealed the signatures were exact duplicates of each other.

Figure 9.8 Cut and paste evidence

Although the placement of each signature relative to the signature line differed, the signatures were determined to be the result of cut and paste.

Since all documents were photocopies, there was no way to know whether two were a duplicate of the third or whether all three were a duplicate of an unknown fourth document.

Because the signature line is in a different place relative to each signature, the signatures were probably removed from a scanned image of the initial document using Photoshop or similar software. The signatures were then placed onto the destination documents.

The person who performed the alteration may have thought the placement of the signature in a different location relative to the signature line would disguise the cut-and-paste, making detection difficult or impossible.

Discover a cut and paste when a source document is missing

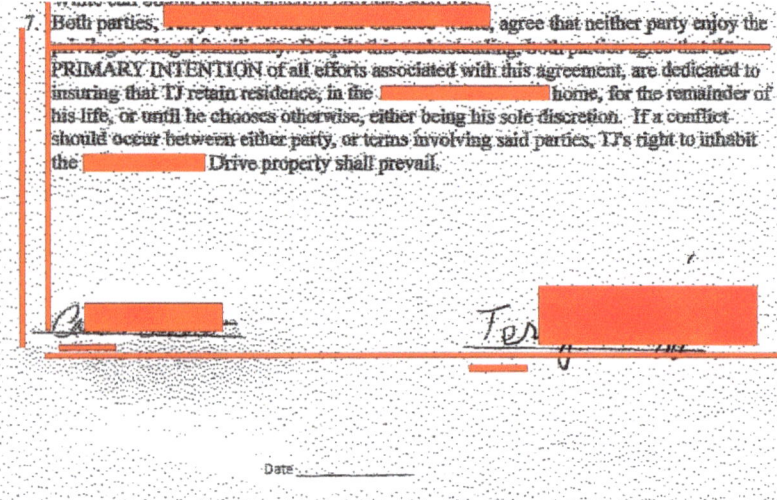

Figure 9.9 Cut and paste without a source file

Generally, a document examiner cannot determine that a signature on a photocopy is cut and paste unless the source signature is available. As stated above, there are exceptions to this rule. When a person is careless creating a document that will be passed as authentic, the document examiner can determine the photocopy is not made from an authentic document.

In a case that went to trial, I demonstrated that a photocopy was created using cut and paste signatures. Attributes of the typed text on the document were compared with the signature lines on the document. Also, the font used for the name under the signature line was compared with the font in the remainder of the document.

A person created a contract, then placed two signatures onto the document. I could not determine whether they were placed onto the page using computer software such as Photoshop, or they were placed onto the page from a manual cutout.

A telltale sign in Figure 9.9 is the signature lines are sloped down to the right for each signature. All the computer printed text on the page was horizontal. If the signature lines were printed on the page with the rest of the printed text, they would have been printed horizontally.

The left-side signature line is indented further right than the bullets in the primary text. This alone does not mean the signature line was pasted onto the contract. It is possible that a person typed leading spaces before starting the signature line.

The signature lines for each person do not align vertically. The signature line on the left side of the page is higher than the signature line on the right side of the page. Had they been printed onto the document, they would align vertically. The vertical distance between the two lines is different from the vertical distance between two of the printed lines of text.

There were many other anomalies on the page, including differences in the font in the names printed below the signature lines and the font in the text of the contract.

The result of the examination is signatures on the contract were not part of the original contract. Therefore, the contract document is not authentic. In this case the source documents for the signatures on the contract were not available. The discrepancies resulted in an opinion the document was created by a cut and paste of the signatures onto the typed document. The mechanism used to place the signatures onto the typed document is unknown.

Alterations using different printers

A set of pages in a document may have been printed on different printers, yet may be part of a true, correct document.

Perhaps text is printed on a laser printer, and the photographs are printed on a photographic printer.

However, if a person does not like the terms of a contract on a specific page, they may retype that page on a computer and change the terms.

The new page might be printed on a different printer using the same font used on the original contract.

The document examiner must be able to determine whether the added page was produced using a different printer.

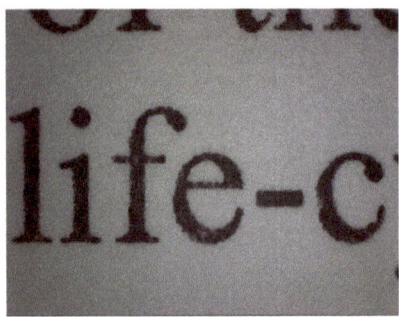
Toner printer

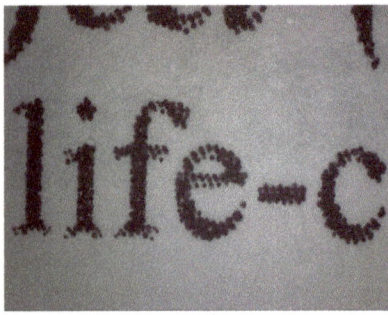
Wax Printer

Figure 9.10 Difference in printers

In Figure 9.10, the word "life-c" is printed on two types of common office printers, the top printer using toner, and the bottom using wax. The fonts are identical for the toner and wax printer examples. The pages appear identical when viewed with the naked eye, but completely different when magnified 40x with a digital microscope.

DETERMINE LINE SEQUENCE FOR POTENTIAL HANDWRITTEN ALTERATION

Determining line sequence means investigating the question, "When two or more lines cross, which line(s) came first?"

A related question is whether someone added a signature over an existing line on the page, or was the signature written before the line was added?

Line sequence is a difficult problem for document examiners to solve.

In cases where the same pen is used, indicators provide the means to determine the stroke sequence. When different pens are used, the problem is often more difficult.

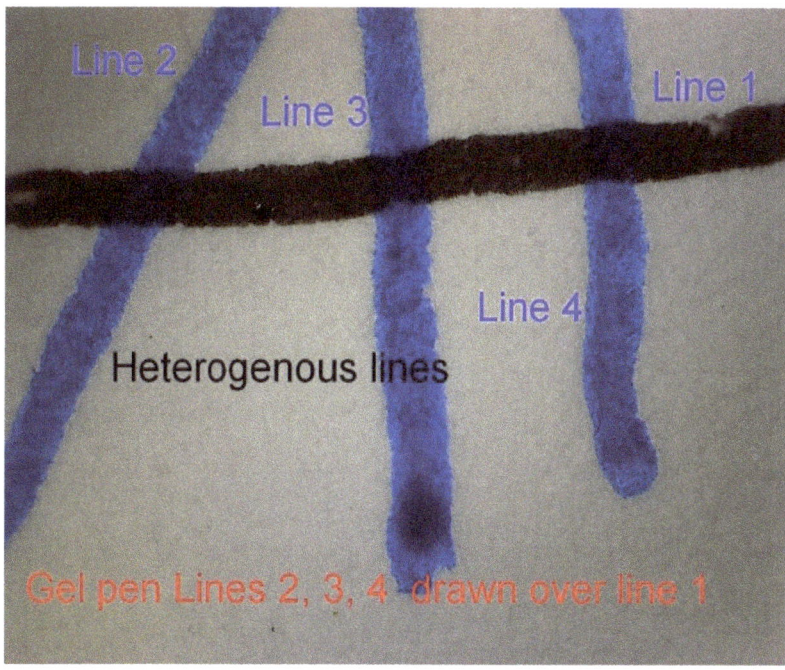

Figure 9.11 Line sequence illusion

I drew the lines in Figures 9.11 through 9.14 to illustrate the difficulty.

Black ink often appears to be on top of blue ink, even when the blue ink is on top. Darker color ink almost always appears on top of lighter color ink. These images were magnified 12 times using a digital microscope.

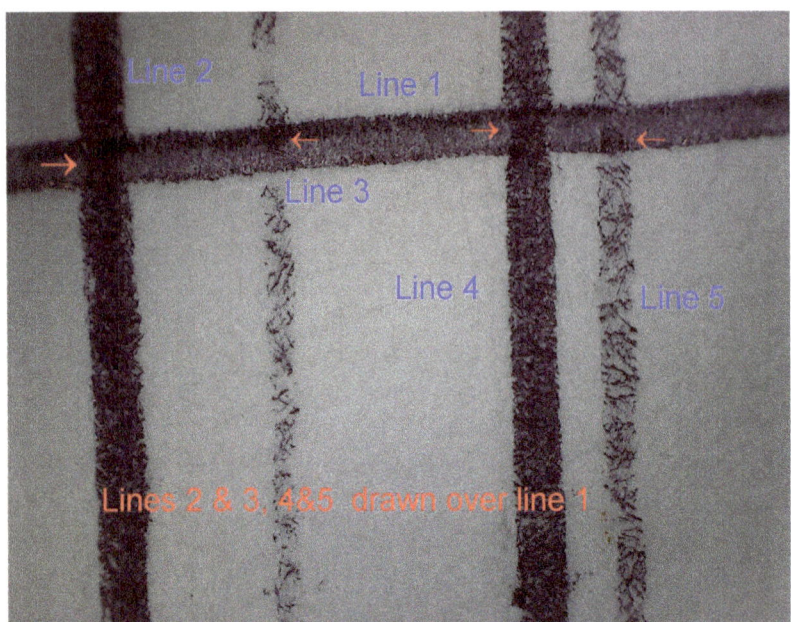

Figure 9.12 Line sequence

In Figure 9.12, using black gel pens, I drew vertical lines 2, 3, 4, and 5 over horizontal line 1.

One indicator is a narrowing of a line, like an hourglass shape shown by the red arrows, where the top line crosses the bottom line.

When the pen crosses the line, it dips into the groove formed by the first pen. This causes the narrowing.

We need to use a microscope to see this, but sometimes the microscope will not reveal the narrowing.

The sequence in which lines were drawn cannot be determined by simply looking at the image. An examiner can try to use alternate light methods to differentiate the inks when two or more of the same color pens were used to alter a document.

As discussed at the beginning of this chapter, our eyes see only a small portion of the electromagnetic spectrum—between approximately 400 and 700 nanometers. Photography using infrared and infrared luminescence allows the document examiner to see beyond that which our eyes can see. If different inks are used, alternate lighting will often reveal the difference.

In Figure 9.13, I used infrared light to view black lines crossing each other.

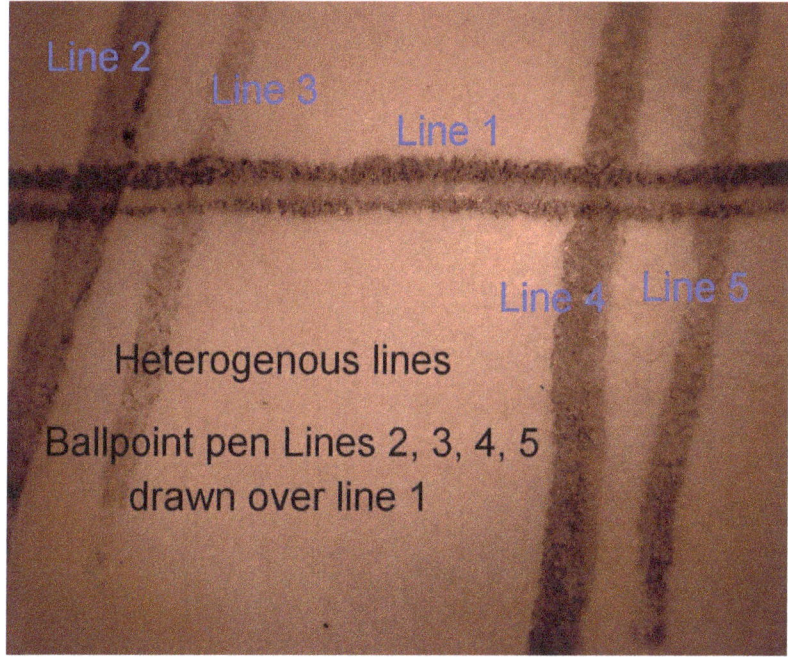

Figure 9.13 Line sequence infrared

This technique does not always work. Note that the horizontal line 1 appears to be on top, even though I drew it prior to drawing the vertical lines.

You can also look for alternate methods such as a narrowing of the line on top. This is seen in line 4 in Figure 9.13

Sometimes two lines may appear to have been made with the same pen when viewed with the naked eye. But infrared luminescence may reveal they were written using distinct inks.

In Figure 9.14, I photographed two black inks using infrared luminescence, which made the inks glow differently.

Figure 9.14 Infrared luminescence

At times, a question may arise whether writing was done with a pen on top of toner or whether the toner was placed over the writing. This question occurs when a person alleges they signed a blank page, and then the page was printed with a signature line or text placed over the signature (yes, this occurs). The allegation is that the person did not sign the page that appears to contain their signature.

Frequently when the ink was written over the toner, the area where the ink and toner intersect appears as a bronze color. This is known as "bronzing". In Figure 9.15 this bronzing appears at the bottom of the "L" and the lower portion of the "N".

At other times, the toner appears lighter at the intersections.

Sophisticated equipment such as the VSC (see Chapter 4) may be needed to reveal these differences in ink and line sequence. Sometimes, even more sophisticated equipment such as a scanning

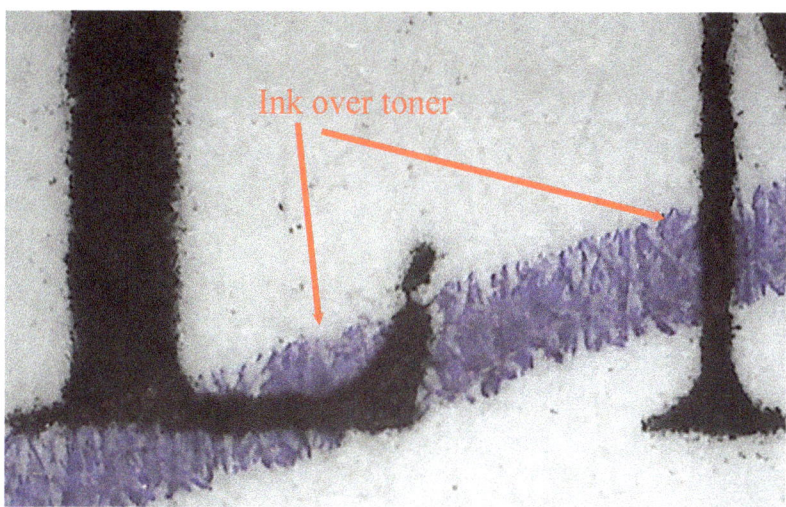

Figure 9.15 Blue ballpoint ink over toner

electron microscope (SEM) that measures the thickness of the lines in nanometers is needed.

Due to cost, university and government laboratories typically own this equipment. When these tests are required, the document examiner may need to engage the services of a specialty laboratory to perform the examination.

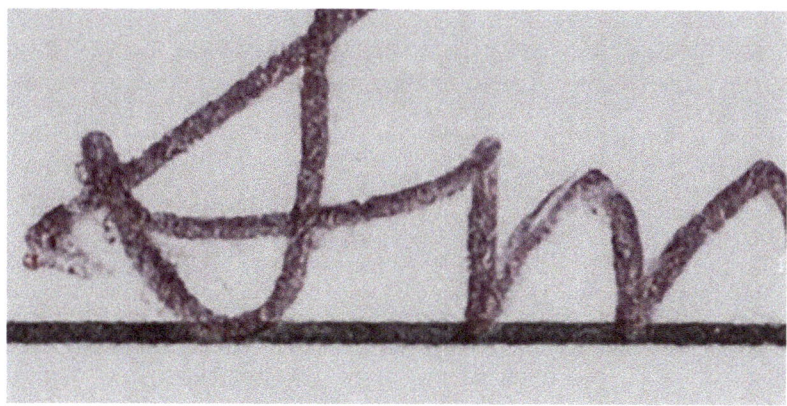

Figure 9.16 Black ballpoint ink over toner

Figure 9.16 demonstrates an example of black ballpoint ink over a black toner line. In this example, the lighter ink line is clearly on top of the horizontal black toner line.

A more difficult question to answer is where the horizontal line crosses the vertical line in the letter "S".

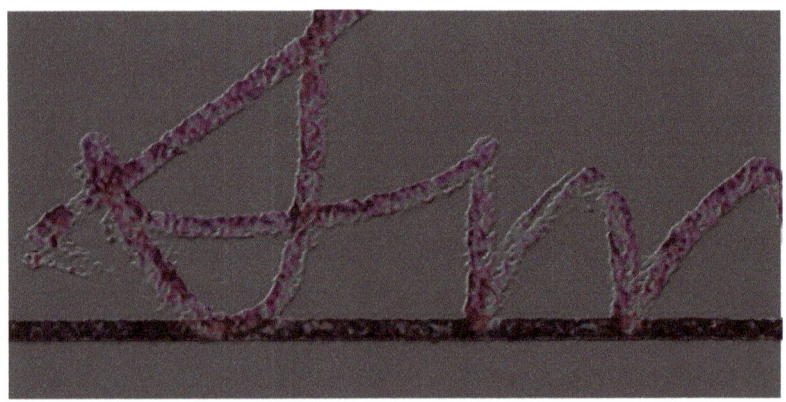

Figure 9.17 The image in Figure 9.16 viewed with NEGA software

Software from a company in Spain assists with determining the sequence of lines. The software called NEGA is a powerful tool used as a digital negatoscope. A negatoscope is used for comparison of x-rays. The software is used by document examiners to determine line sequence. Figure 9.17 shows line sequence of signature in Figure 9.16 as determined by the NEGA software.

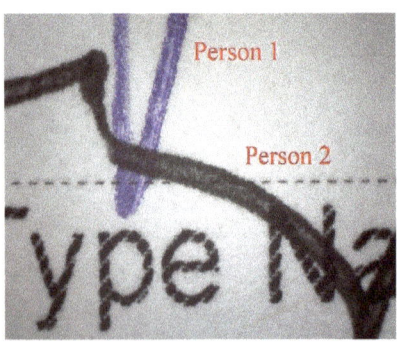

Figure 9.18 Which line came first, white light

The NEGA software is a valuable tool for determining the sequence of ink strokes. There are cases where a document examiner must determine which signature was placed on the page first. Shown in Figure 9.18, a determination needed to be made whether the person one signed the document first or the person two signed the page first. As shown earlier in this chapter, the black line often appears to be on top of the blue line, even if the blue line is on top of the black line. In Figure 9.18 a document examiner cannot tell for certain whether person one or person two signed first. Other techniques must be applied since the techniques described above such as the hourglass narrowing of the second line are not present in this image.

I examined the image in Figure 9.18 with the NEGA software. The purpose was to determine which line came first. The NEGA software has tools for looking at the image in 3-D and highlighting the edges of the writing lines.

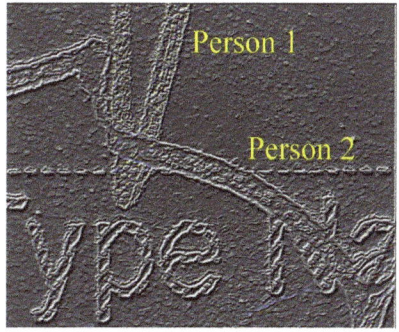

Figure 9.19 Examination of writing with NEGA software

In Figure 9.19, the line written by person 2 crosses over the writing written by person 1. The edges of the person 2 line are visible across the person 1 line. This is also true where the line written by person 2 crosses the letter "N" which shows the ink was applied over the printed text.

EXAMINING TORN DOCUMENTS

I used Photoshop in Figure 9.20 to reconstruct a document that was allegedly a photocopy of a torn document. A person claimed he removed a torn agreement from a trash can and then made a photocopy of the reconstructed document. Only the alleged photocopy of the reconstructed document was provided to my client. The photocopy given to my client is on the top image of Figure 9.20. The reconstructed image is on the bottom image.

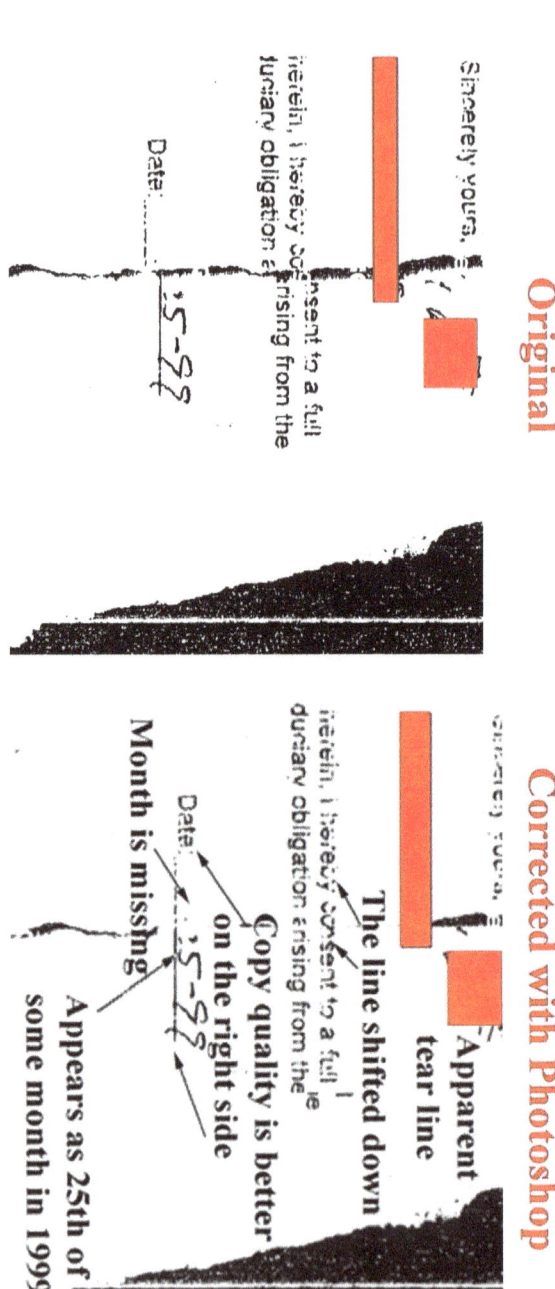

Using Photoshop, I cut the right side of the tear in the document. I moved the right side to align the horizontal line for the date and the type words consent and arising. The result is on the bottom image of Figure 9.20.

I selected the right side of the torn document and aligned it with the left side by aligning the horizontal line for the date and the type words consent and arising. Once aligned, the printed portions matched. But his deception was revealed because regarding the date, there was writing on the right section but no writing on the left section.

INK DATING

Questions arise on whether a document was manufactured for fraudulent purposes. A legitimate document may have been altered by the same person who wrote the original document. In this event, examination of the handwriting may not serve to determine whether the document was altered.

However, a chemical examination of the ink may help determine when the writing was applied to the document. A question may be whether the ink existed at the time the writing was allegedly produced. Another question may be how long ago the ink was applied to the paper.

The document examiner can consult an ink chemist to perform a chemical or spectral analysis to determine the chemical composition of the ink. The composition can be compared to information provided by ink libraries, enabling the identification of the manufacturer and time range that the ink was manufactured.

This technique is valuable to discover whether the ink existed when the document was signed. If a document is dated 1998, yet the ink was not manufactured until 2005, it proves that the document was back-dated.

An ink chemist may also discern approximately when the ink was applied to the paper by analyzing the type and composition of the ink and paper.

PAPER DATING

At times, a document examiner must consult a paper specialist to determine the age of the paper. Paper manufacturers insert watermarks into some paper. Common copier and printer paper rarely contain watermarks. Different papers also have identifying fiber content based on the type of trees and location of the forest from which the paper was produced. These factors are useful in identifying the manufacturer and the approximate date range the paper was manufactured.

Another method of determining the date of paper is to look at a watermark. Watermarks are not found typically on bond paper used for photocopy machines and standard printing paper. Watermarks are found on higher and cotton, linen, and other types of higher-end papers.

Figure 9.21 Watermark with a date indicator

While the paper is wet after it has been manufactured, a dandy role embosses the watermark into the paper. Paper manufacturers occasionally change the dandy role used for that paper. Often times the manufacturer will place a mark onto the dandy role indicating when the dandy role was produced and used.

In Figure 9.21 there is a vertical line under the "b" in "fiber." This line indicates when the dandy role was produced. The document examiner can contact the manufacturer of the paper to learn the timeframe when this dandy role was used. Although this does not provide an exact date when the paper was manufactured, it does provide a date range. Therefore, if the document is dated in 2005 and the dandy roll was not manufactured until 2009, the document examiner knows that the document has been backdated.

Photocopiers and laser printers used for alterations
Trash marks

Figure 9.22 Trash Marks

Often photocopiers and laser printers leave behind small dots called trash marks, shown in Figure 9.22. These may be visible only with a microscope and not with the naked eye.

Trash marks are caused by toner or ink deposits. There are several possible sources of trash marks. Examples of sources of trash marks are:
1. Dust or defects on the glass of a photocopier.
2. A defect in the print drum.
3. Excess toner deposited by the print mechanism.

Document examiners assess trash marks to determine whether they appear in the same place on the pages of the document. Marks appearing in the same location indicate that the same copier or printer was probably used to create the pages of a document.

If all pages of a document contain the same trash marks on all pages except a single page, that page may have been created on a different copier or printer than the other pages. Alternatively, it may have been created on the same copier or printer at a different time prior to creation the defect or after the defect was resolved.

When there is a defective drum, the marks may appear every several pages rather than on every page. This is because more than one page is printed by a single rotation of the drum as it turns. For example, if the same trash mark appears on every fourth page, the trash marks are probably the result of a defective drum.

Inaccurate reproduction of a document by a photocopy machine

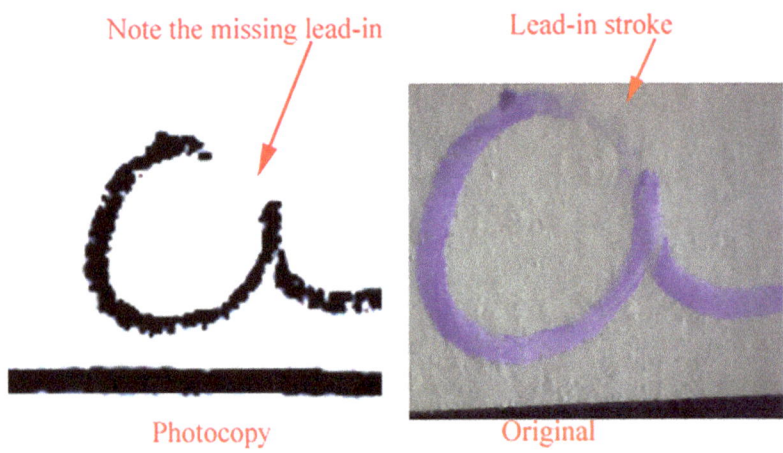

Figure 9.23 Photocopy problems

Photocopy machines may give false impressions about the document when they inaccurately reproduce an image on the document being copied.

For example, Figure 9.23 illustrates what can occur when a portion of an image is written lightly using blue ink. Some photocopy machines may not reproduce the lighter writing.

The original letter "a" in the figure on the right has a very light lead-in stroke which the copier did not reproduce (left side).

In this example, I was first given a photocopy of the questioned document for examination. An anomaly seemed that the writer of the questioned document wrote the letter "a" with an open top. However, when I examined the original questioned document, the light lead-in stroke was visible in the image on the right side of Figure 9.23.

Machine identification code technology in color laser printers

Most manufacturers of color laser printers and color photocopiers that use toner print yellow security markers on each page printed. These security markers are small dots and light color. They are not typically visible when someone is looking at the color photocopy or printed page.

The yellow markers are in the shape of a 15-column x 8-row matrix. The matrix encodes the time the page was printed and the serial number of the printer.

The information provided by the security markers can be valuable to the forensic document examiner when a question arises whether the pages in a document were printed consecutively, or whether the pages were printed on the same printer.

The yellow dots are visible when the document is examined using a microscope. The matrix of dots can be seen when the page is viewed under blue light.

Details for interpreting the matrix can be found on the Electronic Frontier Foundation's website: https://w2.eff.org/Privacy/printers/docucolor/. Marks identify the printer's/copier's make and model and the date when printed.

Photocopied versus original signatures

A microscope may be needed to determine whether a signature on a document is ink or a photocopy of an ink signature.

Dot is not visible in the toner stroke

Dot is visible in the ink stroke

Figure 9.24 Ink Versus Toner

A question may arise when a black ink is used for the signature that looks the same as the black toner used to create the document on which the signature was made. The closeness of the black colors may deceive the eye. The images in Figure 9.24 were made from two pages of a multipage document. A question arose whether the entire document was an original document. The dots are adjacent to the horizontally printed signature line. The images were taken at 140x with a digital microscope then an enlarged three times in Photoshop.

The top image in Figure 9.24 is a photocopy of the signature on a page. This is apparent because the horizontal dot at the left of the visible dot is not visible because it has been created with photocopy toner. All black images on the page are the same color. It is impossible to see images below the signature.

In the bottom image, the signature is original ink. When a different page from the same document is magnified, the dot inside the line is visible below the ink (see the red line pointing to the dot). The printed dot at the lower right of the images is also visible under the ink signature. The result is the page is an original document rather than a photocopy.

The examination demonstrated that in the multipage document, some pages were photocopies and others were original with ink signatures.

Color photocopiers

Figure 9.25 Writing without magnification

Color photocopy machines have improved sufficiently that examination of a photocopied document with the naked eye may not differentiate whether you are viewing an original ink writing or a photocopy of the writing.

The document examiner must examine the writing using a microscope to determine whether the writing is original ink. Figure 9.25 shows a scan at 800 ppi (pixels per inch) (ppi) of an exemplar of a person's signature. To the unaided eye, the writing appears as ink on the page. When the writing is examined using a microscope, the dots that make the color photocopy are apparent in Figure 9.26.

Figure 9.26 Writing with magnification

Figure 9.27 provides another example of color photocopiers' ability to render images that appear to be original documents. This image is a 40x enlargement of a photocopy of a rubber stamp.

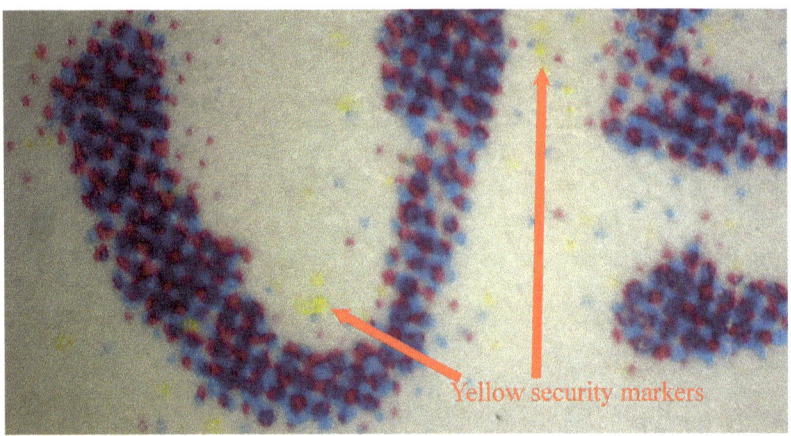

Figure 9.27 Close-up image of a color photocopy

When examined with the naked eye, the page appeared to contain an ink mark from a rubber stamp. However, when the image is enlarged, the small dots that compose the image are apparent.

Here the printer used cyan, yellow, magenta, and black inks to print the images.

The yellow security markers are placed onto the image by the photocopy machine. They show the date and time the page was printed and the serial number of the photocopy machine. This is helpful when there is a question whether all pages of a contract or other document were printed consecutively or on the same machine.

Chapter 10

The future of document examination

Because we are in a digital age, the future of document examination will involve a merger with computer forensics.

Often document examiners are provided documents that were scanned into a computer rather than receiving the original paper documents. They must become proficient at examining computer-generated documents.

To be successful and keep current with court requirements, document examiners must learn to analyze scanned digital images and signatures written on digital signature pads such as the ones used in retail stores. Digital signature pads are also used to sign legal documents, such as insurance forms, real estate forms, notarized forms, etc.

In these cases, an ink signature against which to compare the digital signature is not available. Instead, we have data that was captured by the digital tablet. This begins the merger of forensic document examination with computer forensics.

SIGNATURES ON DIGITAL TABLETS

Figure 10.1 Signature on a digital tablet

Figure 10.1 is an example of a writing written on a digital tablet. This tablet offers the writer no visual feedback on the tablet. The visual feedback for the writing is on the computer screen.

The writing appears somewhat rough because the image is captured by the tablet by requesting data points at regular intervals. Capturing the data is called sampling.

As the pen, or stylus, moves across the surface of the tablet, the location of the stylus on the tablet is recorded. Some tablets sample at 100 times per second, others at 300 times per second, and others at different rates. Sampling is when the tablet senses the location of the stylus.

The writing is stored as data points that can be plotted to display the writing or signature. The software draws a line between each point to present the writing. A mathematical formula may be used to make the signature line looks smooth. When a person writes with a pen on paper, the line is continuous rather than being data points.

Figure 10.2 shows the beginning data points from the writing in Figure 10.1. Since the data points are the same distance in time apart, the document examiner can calculate the time required to execute the writing.

The tablet used to write signature 10.1 captured one data point every 1/100th of a second, or 100 points per second. Due diligence requires the document examiner to learn what type of tablet was used for the writing. This knowledge allows the document examiner to calculate the time required to execute the writing. Therefore, I calculated that the writing in Figure 10.1 was completed in 5.33 seconds since there were 533 points sampled for the signature.

This knowledge takes the subjectivity out of the estimate of speed of writing. When the writing is executed with a pen and paper, the document examiner uses well-established techniques to determine whether the writing was fast, slow, or another description of the speed of writing. With a pen and paper there is no way to calculate a precise speed of writing. Writing on a digital tablet offers more detail in this regard than handwriting with the pen on paper.

388	361
388	360
388	360
388	360
388	359
388	358
387	356
386	355
383	355
378	355
372	356

Figure 10.2
Data Points

The data points in Figure 10.2 can be displayed as a plot of the writing in Figure 10.3. The plot can display important markers at the location of the data points in Figure 10.4 showing how the writing was executed.

Since the tablet samples the data points at a constant rate, the data points show at what portions of the signature the writer writes fast and slowly.

The information in Figure 10.4 enables the document examiner to learn the sequence in which the writing was executed. The long lines between data points are locations where the writer lifted the pen. The dot between the first two long lines or pen lifts is the dot for the "i" in "signature."

Contrary to popular belief, when a person signs a digital tablet, the document examiner may have more evidence on which to base an opinion of authorship than when an ink on paper writing is executed.

Additionally, with the preponderance of digital signatures written on tablets at merchant locations, the document examiner can obtain samples of writing from a person who claims not to have

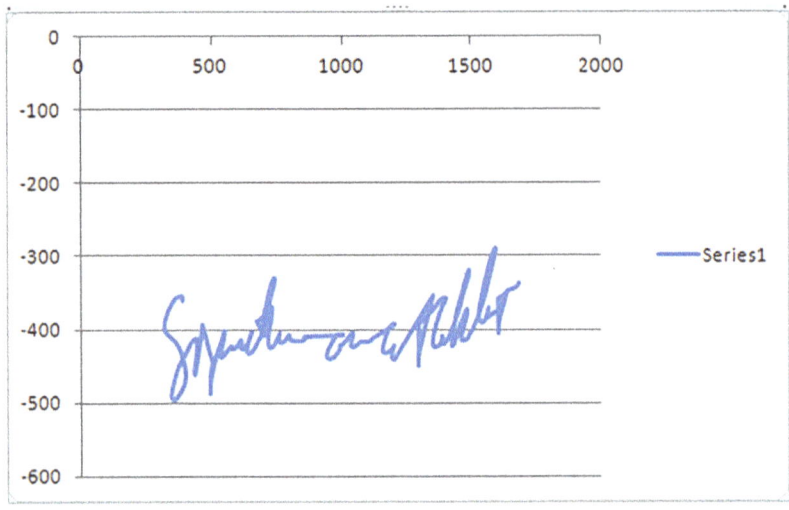

Figure 10.3 Plot of electronically captured writing

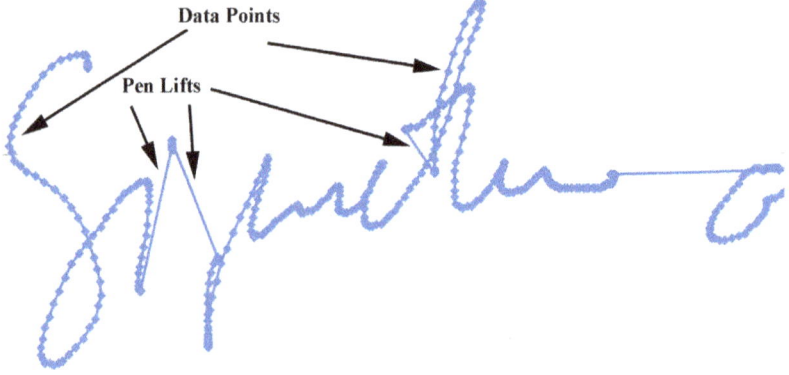

Figure 10.4 Plot of writing showing data points

written a signature or a person suspected of having written a signature. A problem with this approach is that many people sign their name differently on merchant tablets than they do when using pen and paper. This raises the question whether comparison of a signature on a digital tablet is valid for comparison with the signature written on pen and paper.

Due to the differences between continuous signatures on pen and paper and the data points used for signatures created on digital tablets, generally I do not accept signatures from digital tablets as exemplars for signatures written on paper with a pen. When signatures on digital tablets are used as exemplars for ink signatures, a qualified opinion or inconclusive opinion is offered.

The plots of the writing can be compared to learn whether the writing patterns are the same or very similar. This scientific approach removes much of the subjectivity from analyzing signatures.

ELECTRONIC SIGNATURES ON REAL ESTATE DOCUMENTS

There are instances where real estate documents and other type of transactions are signed on digital tablets rather than on paper. In these instances, it is difficult to perform a direct comparison with the exemplars that are written on paper. The same is true when the questioned signature is written on paper and the exemplars are written on the digital tablet. The example below in Figure 10.5, shows a signature that was written on a digital tablet using software called SignNow® from Barracuda software.

Software products that allow a person to write a signature on a digital tablet often offer three different options for placing the signatures on the document. One option is to allow the software to generate the signature out of a cursive font rather than using person's real signature. Another option is to allow the person to write a signature the first time a signature is required on the document. In these instances, the selected signature is placed into each location where the signature is needed on the document. The third option is to allow the person to write a signature each time a signature is needed on the document. The third option most closely resembles how a person would sign many locations on a contractual document.

In many instances, evidence is left on the PDF or JPEG page showing the signature was placed using an electronic format.

Figure 10.5 shows the dotted lines that demarcate the top and bottom of the virtual box in which the electronic signature is placed. Similar evidence is exhibited with signatures executed by DocuSign® software.

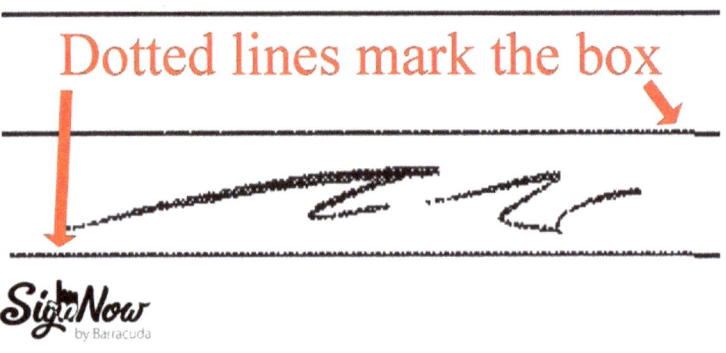

Figure 10.5 Evidence of an electronic signature placed using SignNow

EXAMINATION OF ELECTRONIC DOCUMENTS

Document examiners are often asked to opine on the authenticity of computer-produced, or electronic documents. Examples of these documents are:

1. Portable data files (PDF)
2. Emails
3. Microsoft Word documents
4. Scanned files such as JPEG and TIFF
5. Adobe Photoshop files
6. Many others

Documents created electronically contain metadata. Metadata is data about data. Some aspects of metadata include when was the document created, what computer software was used to create the document, what type of equipment was used to create the document, and many other attributes.

Some of this metadata is displayable by the software used to view the document.

PDF files

Portable data files (PDF) are files that can be read with Adobe Acrobat® or Acrobat Reader®. The advantage of these files is they can be read on almost any type of computing device. The Acrobat Reader software is available for download onto almost any type of computer or mobile device.

Many companies create software that allows for generating PDF files directly from applications such as Microsoft Word, PowerPoint, WordPerfect, and many other commonly used software products. PDF files can be edited using Acrobat Pro software and other third-party software products. It is possible to edit a PDF file without leaving direct evidence that the file has been edited. This is because Acrobat does not have a track changes option that is available in many other software products.

For this reason, evidence that a PDF file has been altered may not be directly visible by simply examining the file.

There are many misconceptions about determining whether the PDF file has been altered. Some people have put forth the assumption that if there are layers in the PDF file, this is evidence of alteration. These layers may be visible using software such as Adobe Illustrator or Photoshop. In many instances, when the PDF file is created directly from another software product such as Microsoft Word, the software creating the PDF creates several sections that are saved as layers.

This is especially true when images are contained within the source document. Depending upon the software used to create the

PDF images may be separated into different layers, giving the impression that they were created in sections then put together. These different layers can also be created when a page is scanned to a PDF file. An example of this misunderstanding is when people read the PDF file of President Obama's birth certificate into Adobe Illustrator and showed there are many layers in the file. These layers were probably created by scanning software.

Figure 10.6 shows an Acrobat Pro tool called Preflight that allows for examination of the separate parts of the PDF file. There is also a software product called PDF CanOpener® from Windjack Solutions that shows the entire contents of the PDF file. The PDF CanOpener program can show in some instances who created some of the images on page of a PDF file.

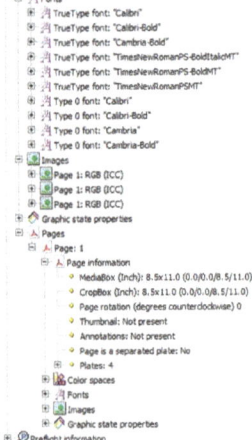

Figure 10.6 Example of Preflight tool in Adobe Acrobat Pro

Figure 10.7 shows metadata stored within a PDF file that can give evidence when the file was created, how the file was created, when it was last modified, and other information.

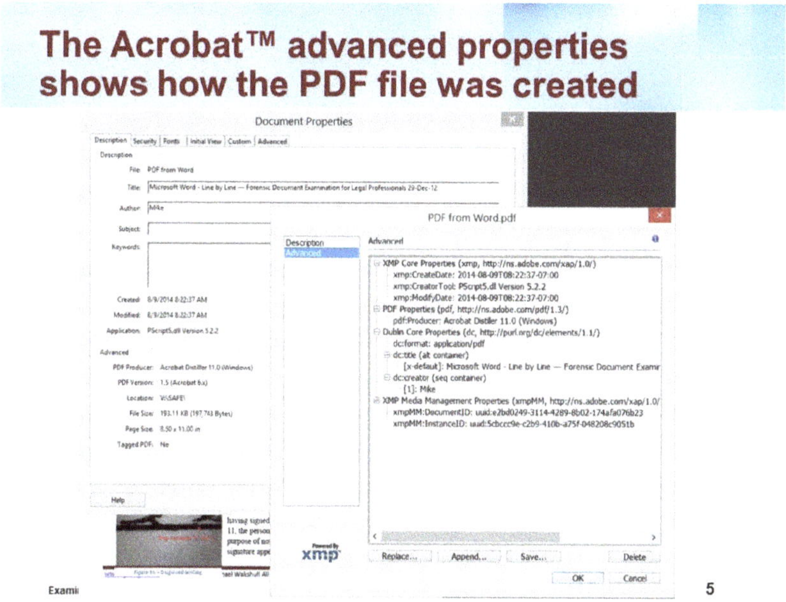

Figure 10.7 Example of Adobe Acrobat metadata properties

Email

Emails contain what's called the message header. This message header shows the source of the email, the route the email took to get from the source to the destination, and much more information about the email.

I had a case in which a person claimed she did not send an email to a coworker. As evidence that the person sent the questioned email to her coworker, the company showed a copy of the email as retrieved by a third-party archiving software product. In my report back to the client, I stated there was no way to know whether the email was actually sent because it was not a printout of Microsoft Outlook. Outlook is the email client used by the company to send emails. My client needed to get a subpoena to examine the Outlook PST file. Since the company was out of state, I turned the assignment over to a computer forensics examiner with software that allows her to remotely, forensically extract the PST file from the company's computer so she could forensically examine the file. Her analysis showed email had been sent from the client's email account at the company. There is no way to know who sent the email as supervisors at the company also had access to this email account.

In another case that required authentication of emails, I only had printouts of screen captures of emails. The question was whether the images represented altered emails. There was no access to the email files on the computer. The client suspected that there were alterations because the fonts appeared to differ in various sections of the emails and among the emails. There was also a question about the indentation of some of the reply emails. When I overlaid the same words from various emails that were allegedly typed using different fonts over each other, I discovered the fonts were identical. Since we were unable to access the actual emails, my opinion was it was inconclusive whether the email chain was altered.

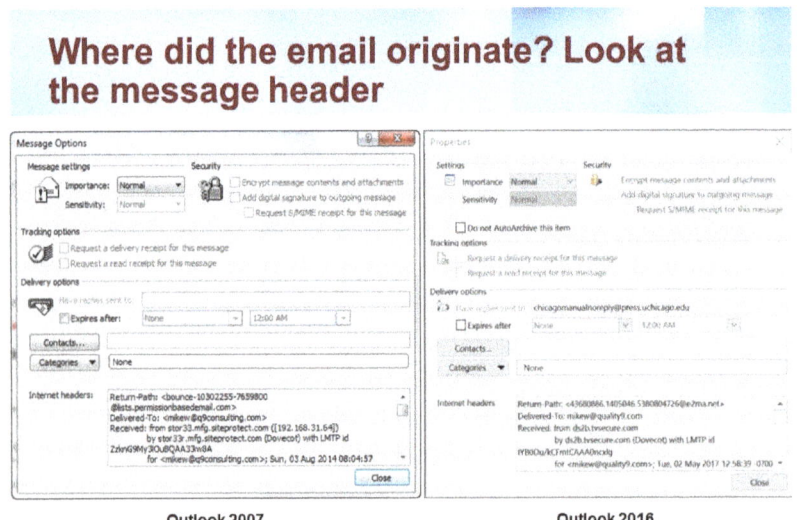

Figure 10.8 Example of email headers in Microsoft Outlook

Figure 10.8 shows examination of email headers using Microsoft Outlook®. All email clients have a method for examination of the header. The left-side image is an example from Outlook 2007. The right-side image is an example from Outlook 2016. The email header shows where the email originated, it's path through the Internet, and the final destination of the email.

Scanned files and photographs

Forensic document examiners often receive images of a document. Frequently these images were created using a digital scanner that saves the file as a JPEG, TIFF, or PDF. Substantial information, or metadata, is usually contained within the digital file created by the scanner.

Figure 10.9 Photograph of a damaged lottery ticket

Using tools such as Adobe Bridge®, or the File Info option within a product such as Photoshop, the document examiner can examine the metadata to learn the date and time the file was created, the type of scanner used to create the document, and potentially the account used to create the document. This is also true of photographs taken with a digital camera. The image in Figure 10.9 shows a damaged California Lottery ticket. My client asked me to retrieve the potentially winning numbers from the damaged ticket. The numbers were not visible to the naked eye.

Digital cameras typically store their files as JPEG or TIFF format. Data such as the f-stop, shutter speed sometimes location where the picture was taken, date and time of the the image photograph, and type of camera used are stored with the photograph. Figure 10.10 displays the metadata for the image in Figure 10.9. The "Basic" tab shows the date and time when the picture was taken

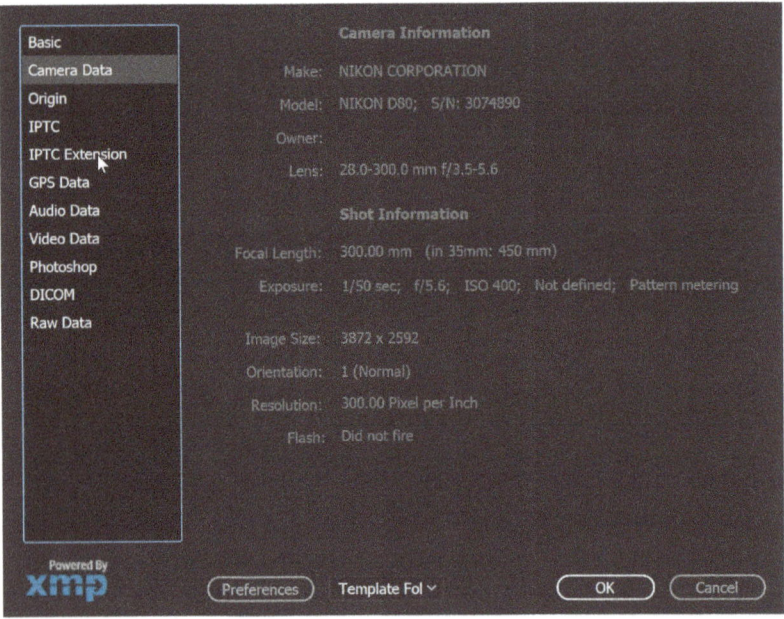

Figure 10.10   Metadata for the image in Figure 10.9

A document examiner may need to engage the services of a digital forensics expert to learn more about the file then is shown in the overt metadata. Digital forensics experts have tools that can show whether the digital image has been modified.

Chapter 11

Standard operating procedures

Each document examiner develops a laboratory procedure best suited for their needs. Regulated industries dictate the standards to be followed. For non-regulated industries, the examiner can follow ASTM/SWGDOC/SAFE or some other industry-recognized standards.

When the document examiner's standard operating procedure (SOP) is based on the ASTM, SWGDOC, SAFE, or other industry recognized standards, and the document examiner follows the SOP, the document examiner is using a generally-accepted practice.

Unlike regulated industries that dictate the standards to be followed, non-regulated industries are not audited to ensure compliance to standards. Forensic document examination is a non-regulated industry.

When audits are performed in regulated industries such as banking or food processing, the auditor examines whether the company is following the stated internal procedures. The internal procedures are audited to determine whether they align with the regulations and standards for the industry.

When a document examiner's standard operating procedures (SOP's) are based on the ASTM/SWGDOC/SAFE standards, the document examiner is using a generally-accepted practice.

The SOP typically describes what the document examiner does when contacted for a new case, how the documents are handled when received, how they are stored and protected, etc. The SOP also describes the standard procedure used to examine documents. It may describe what the examiner looks for during an examination.

The SOP is descriptive rather than prescriptive. The reason is each case is different. Often the examiner must adapt the SOP to the specific case. As an example, the SOP may require the examiner to obtain a minimum of 15 exemplars of the person whose signature is being examined. This sample may prove insufficient for the examiner to reach an opinion other than inconclusive. Here the examiner will request additional exemplars to strengthen the opinion in one direction or the other. In another case the examiner may not be able to obtain 15 exemplars. Upon examination, the examiner may reach an opinion on the authenticity of a signature.

I had a case in which my opinion was a person probably did not sign the document. Additional exemplars were provided. One of the exemplars showed the attribute of the questioned signature that is not in other exemplars. This discovery caused my opinion to change to inconclusive.

EXAMPLE OF A PORTION OF A STANDARD OPERATING PROCEDURE

Step 1: Sort the documents in chronological order

Step 2: Each document is given a unique identifier. The identifier for known documents begins with the letter K followed by a numerical, sequential identifier such as K001. The identifier for the questioned documents begins with the letter Q followed by a numerical, sequential identifier such as Q001.

Step 3: Create a file folder on the computer and in the hardcopy files for the case. Step 3 takes one of two forms:

7. When I receive hard copy (paper) documents I place a sticky note on the paper document, labeling it with the assigned numerical identifier. This enables easy identification of the printed copy of the image. I scan them into the computer with a flatbed scanner using at least 800 pixels per inch (PPI). I store the documents in a tagged information file format (TIFF), which has no loss of resolution due to file data compression. Some document examiners use JPG file format. JPG compresses the data in the file, resulting in loss of resolution. The TIFF is a huge file. A color 8.5" x 11" scanned page at 800 PPI is sometimes more than 175 megabytes in size.

8. Sometimes I receive documents in electronic form such as PDF or JPEG. Images of bank checks typically are scanned images from the bank. I ask the client to send the PDF file, rather than printing the file and sending the printed page to me. The PDF has more detail than the printed image. Sometimes, a client has only an electronic image of a document.

    a. I read the PDF or JPEG files into Photoshop, and then save them as TIFF and Photoshop PSD files with the proper nomenclature. When the PDF file contains several pages, I extract the pages I will use from the file, saving each with the name that identifies the purpose and source. I use Photoshop to annotate the name of the file, such as *K004*, onto the image. An example of a file name is *K004 Jones Trust page 4.*

    b. I rename all other forms of electronic documents with the proper nomenclature and save them into the case folder.

Step 4: Each document is examined for clarity. If the document has not been scanned at a quality that is usable, the document is noted as not usable. If the questioned document(s) are not usable, the analysis cannot be performed.

Step 5: Use Photoshop to extract the writing to be examined from the pages. This procedure removes the background noise such as printed text and other writing. Only the writing being examined, such as a signature and the signature line (if any), remains. Background noise can bias the view of the writing causing the examiner's brain to see patterns that do not exist, or miss important aspects of the writing.

Step 6: For signatures, combine the known writing on as many single pages as required to hold them. This permits examination of the writing for common traits and differences. I then extract the questioned signature from the questioned documents and place it on the page with the known writing. I often change the color of the questioned writing to easily distinguish between the known and questioned signatures.

Step 7: Begin to make the comparisons. Make a copy of the questioned signature to produce an overlay for comparing with the known writing. Change the color of the copy to red.

Step 8: Place the copy of the questioned writing over the known writing to compare the two for similarities and differences.

Step 9: For each known signature, proportionally set the questioned writing to a height that matches the known writing.

This doesn't change the proportions of the writing. Due to variations, research shows that capital letters are not useful for height comparison.

Step 10: When necessary, measure the letters in the writing using the Photoshop ruler tool. Both heights and angles are measured. Export the data to Microsoft Excel for statistical analysis. Statistical analysis software is also used.

When I discover common features in the known writing, I enlarge those features to learn the details of the way the writing strokes were formed. Features such as connections between letters, initial and terminal strokes, and unique idiosyncrasies are examined. I measure relative sizes to determine whether there is consistency in the intra-writer variability.

Essentially, my examination starts at a gross level then works to a more detailed analysis. The gross-level examination is used to determine whether a more detailed analysis is necessary.

The document examiner's SOP includes asking questions of the client to determine the source of the questioned document and exemplars. As an example, the document examiner may need to learn whether the suspected writer of the questioned document had access to the writing instrument used to execute the document.

Summary

Many times, in trial and deposition I've been asked whether I use industry standards for performing the examination. I always state that I use the SWGDOC, SAFE, and/or ASTM standards as appropriate. These standards do not offer a standard operating procedure. They offer guidance on steps for examining a document. A standard operating procedure offers the detail of the applied methodology. When a document examiner follows a standard operating procedure, there is a greater chance that steps will not be missed in the analysis.

Some document examiners state they have a methodology because they use ACE-V (Analysis, Comparison, Examination, and Verification). ACE-V is not a methodology. The methodology is the standard operating procedure that would be used to implement the process.

Chapter 12

Are document examiners better than laypeople at identifying handwriting?

Michael Risinger, law professor at Seton Hall University, and Michael Saks, professor of law at Arizona State University, assert that forensic document examiners may be no better than laypersons at identifying the author of questioned writing. They claim document examination fails the test of applying the scientific method.

They critiqued studies that demonstrate superior ability of trained document examiners to identify or eliminate the author of a questioned writing.

DISCUSSION

Risinger and Saks (1996) discussed the acceptance of expert witnesses in the courts. The 1923 Frye decision at the United States' Supreme Court stated that the methods presented by the expert are judged by the general acceptance of the methods within the scientific community.

The 1993 United States Supreme Court's Daubert decision requires that the expert's presentation must meet specific scientific criteria of falsifiability, or refutability, or testability.

The 1995 United States Supreme Court's Starzecpyzel decision excluded document examiners from the Daubert criteria by classifying document examiners as "skilled experts" rather than scientists. The Starzecpyzel Court stated, "In sum, the Court is convinced that forensic document examiners may be of assistance to you. However, their skill is practical in nature, and despite anything you may hear or have heard, it does not have the demonstrable certainty that some sciences have."

Mary Wenderoth Kelly, the document examiner in the Starzecpyzel case, could not provide quantifiable methods by which to demonstrate differences between writers. The Starzecpyzel Court wrote:

> "If forensic document examination does rely on an underlying principle, logic dictates the principle must embody the notion that inter-writer differences, even when intentionally suppressed, can be distinguished from natural variation. How FDEs might accomplish this was unclear to the Court before the hearing, and largely remains so after the hearing."

The document examination community developed research to demonstrate that document examination, specifically handwriting examination, is a science-based discipline.

Risinger and Saks assert the Starzecpyzel Court was correct in its statement that document examination is not based on science. Risinger and Saks contend that document examination is not a repeatable and verifiable discipline. They attempted to discredit Kam et al.'s (1994) research testing document examiners' ability to identify or exclude the author of a questioned document by using scientifically sound methods.

The basis of handwriting identification is that no two people write exactly alike and the natural variation within an individual's writing is consistent. Risinger and Saks state that handwriting examination is, "not based on standardized measurements of any precision."

Osborn (1929) in chapter VII, "Special Instruments, Measures and Appliances," described several standard measurements. Osborn recognized the need to, "Investigate the question of identity in size, proportions and position in various parts of a model signature and of one or more traced imitations" (p. 83).

Osborn states, "The principle underlying the identification of a handwriting is the same as that by which anything with a great number of possible variations is identified as belonging to a certain class or a particular thing" (p. 225). Osborn concedes writing can be that of another, yet when all the identifying attributes are considered, we can expect that, "it is practically impossible" (p. 226). In other words, when two writing samples have many attributes in common, it is probably the same writer.

Hilton (1993) reiterates Osborn's point stating that identification of a writer is established by identification of sufficient identifying factors as, ". . . their having originated at two different sources is so unlikely that for practical purposes it can be considered nonexistent" (p. 9). Hilton (1995) stated that mathematics is a tool in the scientific approach.

Harrison (1981) wrote, "Where a wide range of identifying characteristics exists, identification can be largely objective, so that opinions as to authorship of handwriting cannot be dismissed as guesses . . . on the part of the document examiner" (p. 292).

Risinger and Saks stated the concept of individuality of each person's writing is "nonscience metaphysical statements" (p. 9). Mary Wenderoth Kelly was unable to provide a standard by which either intra-writer variability or inter-writer variability can be expressed. Risinger and Saks interpret this inability to quantify the variability as metaphysical, or outside the realm of science.

However, this book has shown that both intra-writer variability and inter-writer variability are measurable.

Basing their analysis on the findings of Ms. Kelly, Risinger and Saks state that handwriting identification, ". . . is not based on standardized measurements of any precision."

Osborn (1929) demonstrated the use of precise measures of writing size, slant, spacing and other characteristics to assist with identification. Harrison (1981) described the need to measure the characteristics of writing to distinguish the degree of intra-writer variability.

Srihari et. al. (2002) developed validated measurement techniques to demonstrate individuality of handwriting.

Huber and Hedrick (1999) developed 21 measurable characteristics of writing that together identify the writer. These findings contradict Risinger's and Saks' contention that writing cannot be individually distinguished by using quantifiable and repeatable methods.

CHALLENGES TO THE VALIDITY OF DOCUMENT EXAMINATION

Risinger's and Saks' statement that validation of handwriting identification techniques is not scientific and requires "black box" validation is refutable.

The concept of a "black box" (shown in Figure 12.1) implies that inputs and outputs are known while the processing method

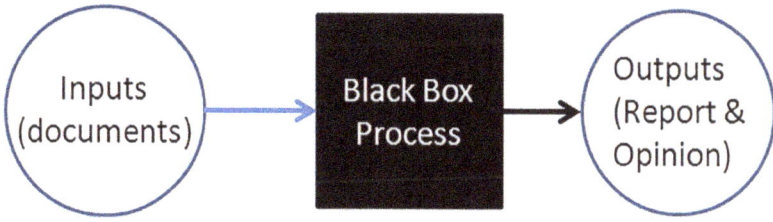

Figure 12.1 Black box process

is unknown. With the document examiner, this implies that the documents to be examined and the report are known, while the method of examination is unknown.

This concept ignores the existence of the wealth of literature and standards, such as the ASTM SAFE and SWGDOC standards, and the LaTrobe University modular methodology that describe methods for examination of documents.

Risinger and Saks asked, "What evidence, if any, exists to show that document examiners can accurately identify or exclude authorship by comparison of hands, or do so better than the average person (p. 10)?" They answered this rhetorical question with, "almost none" (p. 10)."

Stating "almost none" implies there is evidence supporting the contention that document examiners can exclude or identify a writer better than a lay person. Evidence supports the contention that document examiners can exclude or identify a writer better than a lay person.

Risinger and Saks reference a study by Kam et al. (1994). Kam et al. sought to test the results of a 1989 literature search by Risinger et al., which questioned the validity of handwriting examination as a tool for law enforcement and compared handwriting examination expertise to folk medicine and astrology.

Rather than attempting to refute the results of the Kam study based on the experimental design, Risinger and Saks developed a hypothesis that the motivation of the two experimental groups in Kam's study differ.

Kam's test group comprised seven FBI laboratory document examiners. The control group comprised 10 graduate students from Drexel University. Risinger and Saks argue that the control group was less motivated to perform well on the test, thus giving less successful results.

Risinger and Saks failed to show evidence that the subjects' motivation affected the results of the experiment. Kam concluded, ". . . professional document examiners from the Federal Bureau of Investigation are significantly better in performing writer identification than college-educated nonexperts." Risinger and Saks conceded, "The performance of the FBI document examiners was remarkable".

Laboratory error in five tests conducted by the Forensic Sciences Foundation in 1984-1987 is cited by Risinger and Saks.

The inherent error of the laboratories does not support the theory there is no scientific basis for handwriting identification. Risinger and Saks fail to explore the testing methods used by the laboratories. Without this information, drawing a valid opinion regarding the results is not possible.

A comparison must be made of the methods yielding a correct result and those resulting in an erroneous result. By failing to explore test methods, Risinger and Saks support their contention that document examination is a "black box."

Results from the National Academy of Sciences

In 2009 the National Academy of Sciences issued a report calling for a more scientific approach to forensic sciences (National Research Council, 2009). Forensic document examination was included in the report.

In essence, the report stated that use of subjective methods and laboratory bias has yielded incorrect results in the forensic disciplines. This statement supports Risinger's and Saks' observation that a scientific method must be applied to document examination. Conversely, it does not support the hypothesis that document examiners do not use scientific methods.

Subjective analysis by document examiners can yield incorrect results. This is shown by the difficulty document examiners had differentiating simulated and disguised writing (Found and Rogers, 2008).

Found and Rogers stated, ". . . the misleading rate for the disguise category of questioned signatures is very high due to the strategy of observing dissimilar features and concluding this equates to a different writer". The results of Found and Rogers do not purport that document examiners do not use a scientific method. It shows the need for refinement of the methods applied in a specific type of examination.

Found and Rogers (2008) reported the study that was performed with qualified document examiners resulted in ". . . a correct called (CC) percentage of 92.2% and a misleading called (MC) percentage of 7.8%" (p. 56).

Dyer et. al. (2006) conducted a study to examine the strategy used by trained document examiners and lay people when examining signatures. The control group (lay people) was trained for 30 minutes on signature analysis. Dyer reported, ". . . that FDE [Forensic Document Examiner] subjects perform significantly better on signature tasks than do lay people".

The document examiners were shown to apply better cognitive skills and focus on the significance and weight of features rather than focusing on single features as did the lay subjects. Dyer demonstrated a repeatable and quantifiable approach used by document examiners.

In Crisp (2003), the Fourth Circuit Court of Appeals ruled, "The fact that handwriting comparison analysis has achieved widespread and lasting acceptance in the expert community gives us the assurance of reliability that *Daubert* requires".

Denbeaux and Risinger (2003) ignored this ruling in their presentation of a brief history of the admissibility of handwriting expertise in the courts. Referring to appellate decisions on handwriting evidence, Denbeaux and Risinger wrote, "The appellate decisions all managed to find no abuse of discretion without describing the particular claim of expertise which was at stake in the case".

Chapter 13

Document examiners must meet legal standards

FEDERAL RULES OF EVIDENCE RULE 702

Experts in the United States must meet two basic legal standards to qualify to testify in court: 1) Federal court: Federal Rules of Evidence 702. 2) State courts: Each state has its own code.

FRE Rule 702 states:

"A witness who is qualified as an expert by knowledge, skill, experience, training, or education may testify in the form of an opinion or otherwise if:

(a) the expert's scientific, technical, or other specialized knowledge will help the trier of fact to understand the evidence or to determine a fact in issue;
(b) the testimony is based on sufficient facts or data;
(c) the testimony is the product of reliable principles and methods; and
(d) the expert has reliably applied the principles and methods to the facts of the case."

These requirements are restated in ASTM/SWGDOC Standard E444, Scope of Work of Forensic Document Examiners.

ASTM standard E2388 / SWGDOC standard, Minimum Training Requirements for Forensic Document Examiners provides a syllabus for the training and education needed by forensic document examiners.

FRYE V. UNITED STATES

In the 1923 case, Frye v. United States, 54 App. D.C. 46, 47, 293 F. 1013, 1014 (1923), the United States Supreme Court stated that expert opinion based on a scientific technique is inadmissible unless the technique is "generally accepted" as reliable in the relevant scientific community.

The Frye Court wrote, ". . . while courts will go a long way in admitting expert testimony deduced from a well-recognized scientific principle or discovery, the thing from which the deduction is made must be sufficiently established to have gained general acceptance in the particular field in which it belongs."

Many states, including California, apply the Frye standard for admissibility of experts. These states recognize that the judge cannot have sufficient knowledge of every discipline to determine whether the expert is truly knowledgeable of the subject matter to act as a gatekeeper. Frye requires the expert to apply generally accepted practices.

Although the Frye Court addressed, ". . . admitting expert testimony deduced from a well-recognized scientific principle or discovery," the opinion also addressed admissibility of, "the opinions of experts or skilled witnesses." The Starzecpyzel Court ruled that document examiners are "skilled experts."

In the November 26, 2012 ruling in Sargon Enterprises, Inc. v. University of Southern California, the California Supreme Court cited Daubert and FRE 702 in excluding the testimony of a business valuation expert as being speculative in estimating potentially lost profits.

Writing the unanimous opinion, California Supreme Court Justice Ming Chin wrote, "The trial court properly acted as a gatekeeper to exclude speculative expert testimony. Its ruling came within its discretion." Without adopting the Federal Rule 702 or Daubert standard, the California Supreme Court took a step in the direction of the judge as gatekeeper and moving away from Frye. Judge Chin cited Rule 702 in his opinion. Without adopting the Federal Rule 702 or Daubert standard, the California Supreme Court stepped toward the judge as gatekeeper and moving away from Frye.

The Sargon decision focused on the validity of the methodology used by the forensic expert. Here the expert developed an estimate of lost profits based on belief rather than prior history. The court ruled the expert's opinion was inadmissible.

As stated earlier, a trial judge reminded me that Frye does not apply to my discipline because document examiners are not scientists. If you are in a state that applies Frye for acceptance of expert testimony, the judge's interpretation of Frye may determine whether your expert's testimony is accepted.

DAUBERT V. MERRILL-DOW PHARMACEUTICALS

In 1993, the case Daubert v. Merrill-Dow Pharmaceuticals was decided by the United States Supreme Court. The case defined the requirements for expert testimony.

- Has the scientific theory been tested?
- Has the scientific theory been peer reviewed and published?
- What is the potential error rate?
- Do standards and controls exist and are they maintained?
- Has the theory and body of knowledge been generally accepted in the relevant industry?

The Daubert ruling was applied to Federal Rules of Evidence §702.

Applying the scientific method

Many people, including many experts, are unclear about the definition of the scientific method, which can be used to your advantage in court. In January 2016, the National Commission on Forensic Science published a report, "Testimony Using the Term 'Reasonable Scientific Certainty'." The Commission wrote, "the term 'reasonable degree of scientific [or discipline] certainty' has no place in the judicial process."

The scientific method requires the expert to establish a hypothesis and then conduct empirical tests to determine the validity of the hypothesis.

The Daubert court cited authorities stating, "'The criterion of the scientific status of a theory is its falsifiability, or refutability, or testability.'"

Testing the refutability of a hypothesis means we try to disprove rather than prove the hypothesis. This is because attempting to demonstrate that the hypothesis is correct may cause a confirmation bias. Confirmation bias means the investigator focuses on information confirming the hypothesis and rejects information conflicting with the hypothesis.

The expert must also show that the methodology used to arrive at an opinion can be tested and repeated by others. The theories applied to the research methodology should have been published in peer reviewed journals demonstrating that other people in the field have said this is an acceptable methodology.

The next question of error rate is difficult for document examiners to determine. The error rate referenced in Rule 702 is the error rate of the methodology used. Since most document examiners follow their own methodology, it is difficult to know the error rate of a methodology in the industry. What is a document examiner's error rate? Even when an SOP is based on an industry standard, the steps in the SOP are not uniform across document examiners.

Even if the document examiner only considers their own methodology, unless there is a stated and documented standard operating procedure there is no way to know whether the methodology was always properly followed.

Another difficulty with knowing the error rate of a methodology is the question of how to know whether the results were correct. Unless a suspect acknowledges having written the questioned writing or having altered a document, the document examiner does not have constructive knowledge whether the opinion reached was correct.

Document examiners can take proficiency tests to determine performance on a controlled test. Performance on one or even a few tests does not set the standard for error rates. If a person correctly answers 95 percent of the answers on a test, this is the error rate for the test. It is not necessarily reflective of overall performance. The same is true if a person scores 80 percent on a test. The person may solve all answers correctly on another test.

I took a standard proficiency test offered by an independent testing organization for Forensic Document Examination. I earned a perfect score. A perfect score was earned by 203 of the 215 test takers: almost 95% of the test takers scored a perfect score. Based on these overall results I wonder how representative the test is of actual case work.

University studies have been conducted to ascertain error rates of document examiners versus lay people when examining signatures. The question whether controlled studies are equivalent to field performance has not been answered.

Huber and Hedrick (1999) address the question of error rate by examining the likelihood ratio. A difficulty with this approach is determining the frequency of occurrence in an overall population.

U.S. versus Starzecpyzel stated document examination is not a science because of the difficulty in determining error rates.

Document examination was ruled as not a science. It does not have published error rates and is not published in journals of pure science. Document examination was not subject to Daubert.

Kumho Tire versus Carmichael 526 U.S. 137 (1999) ruled expert testimony must follow proper technique. The court ruled Daubert applies to all expert testimony, not just scientific testimony.

The judge is given flexibility in allowing acceptance of expert testimony. Therefore, forensic document examiners are subject to the Daubert standards when testifying as an expert witness in federal court.

ISSUES WITH THE ERROR RATE REQUIREMENT

Daubert requires knowledge of "known or potential error rate for the methodology used." The document examiner needs to be able to quantify the potential errors. A problem with the error rate requirement is that the term error rate is not defined.

Potential definitions of error rate include, but are not limited to:
1. The total number of errors made in a specific case.
2. The average number of errors made across all cases.
3. The average number of cases in which at least one error was made.
4. The median number of cases in which at least one error was made.
5. The total number of cases in which at least one error was made.

Other questions regarding the error rate include:
1. What is the degree of error?
2. Does the error cause the case to be decided in the wrong direction or is it immaterial?

Types of error rate:
1. False positive where a person who should be eliminated is incorrectly identified as a writer or an altered document is identified as authentic.
2. False negative where a person who should be identified as a writer is incorrectly eliminated as the writer, or an authentic document is acknowledged as not authentic.
3. A combination of false positive and false negative.

In the case of number 3, the document examiner would need to report how often the methodology yields an error in either direction.

Different interpretations of error rate can be applied to different situations, adding to the ambiguity surrounding error rate.

Identification of potential sources of errors and results of errors are often subject to interpretation the individual reporting the errors. A standard methodology must be established across the discipline to ascertain the error rate for a methodology.

The opportunity for error depends on the total number of samples, or exemplars, collected. Document examiners use exemplars of known writing to look for variability in the writing as well as unique attributes in the writing.

When a small number of exemplars are collected, there is less opportunity to discover attributes of the questioned writing in the known writing samples.

As the sample size of exemplars increases, the chance of finding unique anomalies of the questioned writing in the known writing increases.

When anomalies in the known writing writings are not found in the questioned writing, a larger sample size of exemplars increases the confidence that they were not written by the same person.

Regardless, there remains an opportunity to err when stating that the writings are from two or more individuals when anomalies found in the questioned writing are not found in the known writing.

The quality of the exemplars may be a source of error. In one case, unknown to me, I was given the questioned document after the fingerprint examiner processed the document with the chemical compound Ninhydrin.

I opined the toner from the printer was on top of the ink-written signature. When I saw the images taken by the opposing examiner, my opinion was corrected. The opposing examiner photographed the document prior to its being processed by the fingerprint examiner. I could see that the ink was on top of the toner. The Ninhydrin washed the ink from the toner.

When errors are reported, the root cause of the error must be discovered. Simply stating that an error occurred offers no insight to the resolution of the error. The source may be the methodology or it may be the person's interpretation of the methodology.

Many variables contribute to error rate. If the question is," What is the average error rate?" the answer may not reflect the actual error rate for the methodology given the specific circumstances.

Average is a poor statistic. As an example, assume a document examiner makes one error per 10 cases worked, or an average total error rate of 10 percent. When the document examiner works on 20 cases, how many errors will be made? The correct answer is, "We cannot predict the number of errors the document examiner will make, if any. Nor can we predict the case in which an error will be made."

Stating the error rate for a methodology across examiners is also of little value when considering a specific forensic document examiner. The error rate for the population is unlikely to apply to any specific person.

Asking an examiner for their error rate is an ambiguous question. Most cases settle without a court adjudication. When a case does go to court, the document report is often only one point that influences the trier of fact's ruling.

For example, I testified as to the authenticity of the signature on a will. Although the court agreed with my opinion regarding the decedent's signature, the court ruled against the side that retained me because the will did not meet California probate code requirements.

In another case, in its opinion the court agreed with me, but the attorney who retained me lost the case because the plaintiff convinced the court he was high on drugs at the time the contract was executed, so he did not have capacity to contract.

When the Court sides with the document examiner or rules in favor of the opinion of the opposing document examiner, it does not mean a document examiner's opinion is right or wrong. It means the prevailing document examiner presented the evidence in the most compelling manner, or there may be other defects in the case.

Even when the document examiners on both sides of the case agree, it does not prove that both arrived at the correct opinion.

Stating whether an opinion is in error implies the ability to know with certainty whether the opinion is correct or not correct. In document examination, absolute certainty can never be stated.

Occasionally the truth can be determined because a person confesses to having written a signature, made alterations, or other statements.

In most instances, the document examiner never learns the results of a case. When an attorney reports that the settlement was enhanced because of the document examiner's report, this still states no error or lack of error by the document examiner. It only means the report was sufficient to cause the other side to realize the weakness of their case.

There are document examiners who report their error rate is zero! This is an absurd claim. Their claim is based on obtaining a score of 100 percent on proficiency examinations. Proficiency examinations are controlled examinations offered by companies such as Collaborative Testing Services and ST2AR. These examinations are not necessarily reflective of real cases worked by document examiners. The results of a few tests are not reflective of all real-world cases.

At a conference, I participated in an exercise where we had to sort the writings of unique writers from a stack of approximately 60 writings. One of the members of my group had claimed a zero percent error rate. We did not get all the answers correct. His claim of zero errors was proven false.

I took a recent proficiency test offered by a national testing service for forensic document examination. Not only did I obtain a score of 100 percent, but almost 95 percent of people who took the test scored 100%. The testing service shows the overall results when it delivers the individual results to the test-taker.

Summary for error rate

When asked, "What is the error rate of a methodology?" a document examiner must first know the definition of error rate. On what criteria is the question based?

Controlled experiments such as proficiency tests and academic studies have returned results.

Proficiency tests are not scientifically based since the subjects are self-selected rather than randomized. The tests are not necessarily representative of the cases a document examiner receives in normal practice. The methodology used by each test taker is not known by the examiner who took the test.

Academic experiments may be more properly controlled than proficiency tests. Yet a question exists as to the selection process for the subjects.

- Are the subjects volunteers?
- What is the criteria for selecting the subjects from the set of volunteers?

In either setting a question arises on the methodology used to solve the test cases. Unless a scripted methodology is used, the results may not speak to the reliability of any methodology, as different subjects may apply individualized methodologies to solving the problem.

As to the definition of error, if a document examiner opines, "The writer of the known documents *probably* wrote the questioned document" and subsequently the subject confesses to having signed the questioned document, did the document examiner err? The proper opinion would have been, "The writer of the known documents is *identified* as the writer of the questioned document."

Until the word *error* is properly defined and knowledge of the true state of nature for the questioned document is known, error rate cannot be properly stated.

Chapter 14

Can forensic experts overcome their biases?

None of us wants to feel our opinions are tainted by bias. The ability to recognize when bias is an influence in an expert's opinion and the skill of an expert to overcome his or her biases is integral to an expert's credibility.

Experts make decisions that are expressed as opinions by applying analytical methods developed through training, education and practice. Such prior experience may induce biases that cause the expert to use trusted methods without considering alternatives.

Forensic science seeks to produce reliable evidence which is clearly reported (Sjerps & Meester 2009). Experts must recognize when their biases and those of others influence their decisions.

WHAT IS BIAS?
Black's Law Dictionary Ninth Edition defines *bias* as, "A predisposition to decide a cause or an issue in a certain way (Garner, 2009)." Black's Law Dictionary Tenth Edition defines bias as, "A mental inclination or tendency; prejudice; predilection (Garner, 2014)." Prior experiences, learning paradigms, individual beliefs, and other biases can cloud the understanding of what is important.

There are two types of bias: cognitive bias and motivational bias (Giannelli, 2008). Cognitive biases, which occur at the subconscious level, frequently interfere with people's ability to make good decisions. Motivational bias, which can occur at the conscious or subconscious level, results from a person's desire to deliver expected results.

Black's Law Dictionary Tenth Edition (Garner, 2014) offers six types of courtroom bias.

1. *Actual bias* occurs when "Genuine prejudice that a judge, juror, witness, or other person has against some person or relevant subject" is present. Examples of this bias are when a person believes that a member of an ethnic, racial, political, or other group possesses certain behavioral traits. Actual bias may cause a trier of fact to believe or not believe that a person committed a certain act.

    Example: In one case, the judge advised the litigants that when he was in private practice he often worked with the opposing document examiner. The attorney who retained me did not object to the relationship. In his ruling, the judge referenced his preference for the opposing examiner's testimony due to his prior knowledge of the examiner's work.

2. *Advocate's bias* is present when an advocate for a person or cause becomes too involved with the person or cause being advocated. As an attorney, your job is to advocate for your client's case, whether or not you believe the client is guilty of the charges or claims. The retained expert is an advocate for the evidence rather than for a party to the case. When an attorney becomes too involved with a case, advocate's bias may develop, causing the attorney to make mistakes and overlook important issues.

    Example: In a case where I was retained by the defense, the plaintiff alleged she had not signed several documents.

My analysis confirmed she had not signed two or three of the seven questioned documents. Although my testimony would not benefit my attorney client, she wanted me to testify at trial. Had she become too much involved with the case?

3. *Implied bias* can result from relationships among parties. The expert witness must avoid any implied bias by receiving full payment for services prior to offering testimony. The implied bias is that the expert is testifying in a particular manner to ensure receipt of payment. Another form of implied bias occurs when the expert has a relationship with a party to the case. Implied bias is also known as *presumed bias*.

4. *Presumed bias* is the sixth type of bias mentioned in Black's Law Dictionary.

5. *Inferential Bias* is when a potential jurors bias does not rise to the level of implied bias.

    Example: A friend is a true crime writer. She was called for jury duty in a criminal case. During voir dire she was asked whether she had any knowledge of any of the defendants. She knew of one of the defendants because she had written about him in one of her books. She also disclosed that she had written about the judge in one of her books. She was selected as an alternate juror for the case.

6. *Judicial bias* occurs when the judge or trier of fact has a bias for one party in a case. Judicial bias may take the form of any other type of bias.

    Example: In one case, the opposing side asked permission from the judge to depose me as I was called to testify. This was on day ten of the trial. The reason given was that they had not taken my deposition after I saw the original signed questioned document. Permission was granted. I was deposed in the afternoon, then testified at trial on the following morning.

I created a PowerPoint slide set showing demonstrative exhibits of the results of examining the original document. This slide set was presented in trial, along with a hardcopy printout for the trial participants to review as I testified.

A few days after my testimony, I asked my retaining attorney status of the case. She stated the judge was favoring the other side because he had forgotten that I examined the original document. The judge said the other document examiner examined the original and I had examined only a photocopy. I suggested she remind the judge the reason my testimony was delayed for a day was so I could be deposed about my examination of the original document and I testified for five hours about the original.

Had the judge already made up his mind regarding the outcome of the case before my testimony on day ten? Had he not listened to my testimony?

LABORATORY BIAS

Document examiners work in private, crime, or other forms of laboratories. ASTM reported that 80 percent of studied laboratories showed laboratory bias (Lawrey, 2009). Twenty percent of the laboratories displayed "significantly high bias."

This bias resulted from interactions among many people.

Griffen and Tversky (1992) attributed similar bias to people's tendency to be more overconfident in their judgments than is warranted by the facts. "When we select evidence that is not independent of the forensic analysis, problems occur" (Sjerps & Meester, 2009). The forensic examiner must avoid information that is not relevant to the forensic analysis. This information may bias the examination or the opinion reached by the examiner. Schwab (2008) showed that bias induces experts to be overconfident in rating their abilities.

BIAS IS EVER-PRESENT

The National Academy of Sciences (NAS) (National Research Council, 2009) reported that bias is a severe problem in forensic sciences. Cognitive biases were described as "common features of decision making, and they cannot be willed away."

NAS reported that judges are subject to bias in their rulings. The NAS report cites studies showing that bias had been introduced in half the fingerprint examinations.

NAS recommended removing crime laboratories from police agencies to reduce the motivational bias of forensic examiners to opine in favor of the prosecution. A common problem is when the prosecution presents evidence to the crime laboratory then states that the evidence was found in the possession of a crime suspect.

NAS recommends using an independent laboratory that examines evidence for both the prosecution and the defense. In this manner the laboratory examiners are not told who provided the evidence. They are only told the scope of the examination.

For example, the document examiner may be requested to determine the authenticity of a signature provided with exemplars. If no information was given to the examiner whether the person wrote or did not write the signature, the expert's bias can be reduced. Bias is reduced when the expert is not aware of the side which has hired them (Baer, 2005).

According to research, awareness of the source of cognitive bias is insufficient to prevent a person from being trapped by biases (Ariely 2008, Cialdini 2001).

A study by Arzy et al. (2009) discovered that by including one misleading detail about a patient, the misdiagnosis rate by practicing physicians in emergency room cases was 90 percent. Informing a control group that there was one misleading detail did not reduce the diagnostic error. When the misleading detail was omitted from the information, the misdiagnosis was reduced to 30 percent.

Document examiners must sort through evidence to avoid following a trail of misleading information which results in a flawed opinion.

For example, sometimes the retaining attorney offers the examiner details about the case that are not pertinant to the document examination. Details such as a confession, witness's statement, or the place where the document was discovered may unconsiously bias the document examiner's perception of the authenticity of the document in question. For this reason, it is best not to provide details about the case when hiring your expert.

CONTEXTUAL BIAS

Research shows that document examiners who work for the government tend to focus on similarities in writing, whereas private practice document examiners tend to focus on differences in writing (McAlexander, 1999).

This is because government examiners typically are retained by the prosecution, whose emphasis is to convict the accused. The private examiner is typically retained by either a public defender or private defense counsel, whose focus is to exonerate the accused party. Each case provides an example of contextual bias.

Knowing the context encourages bias

Research shows when a person is exposed to a concept, they anchor to the concept at a subconscious level. Being exposed to the context of a case causes the document examiner to anchor to that context.

Anchoring is the psychological tendency to set the given context as the starting point for thinking. For example, when a person sees the price of a product, that price becomes the anchor from which they judge the price shown for the product by other merchants.

Document examiners arrive at an opinion whether a document is authentic or not authentic. Bias can come into play when the context is brought to the expert's attention.

Bias begins at the outset

The bias begins when document examiners are hired by an attorney. The attorney approaches the document examiner saying, "I have a case where my client claims he did not sign this check," or "my client claims she did not sign this contract."

These statements set the foundation for cognitive, or subconscious bias.

One of the jobs of a document examiner is to disengage from the bias. This can be accomplished by taking a step back from the scope of the attorney's examination request and focusing on the evidence. Applying an objective scientific approach reduces cognitive bias.

How to reduce bias

A person is incapable of writing beyond their highest skill level. Literacy level may be important when comparing a written text with a questioned letter or other written text. A document examiner may review the document for typographical or grammatical errors to determine the potential educational or literacy level of the writer.

In a case where the skill level demonstrated in the questioned document exceeds that of the known writings, a valid opinion is that different people wrote the documents. Such comparisons help reduce potential contextual bias.

You should find that your document examiner is disinterested in the details of your court case. The less information you provide to the examiner, the more objective the results will be.

The only point of interest is the documents. Specifics of the origin or history of the documents may be requested by the document examiner, but remember that too much knowledge may induce cognitive or unconscious bias.

Approximately 100 years ago Dr. Julius Fischhof, a Hungarian document examiner, recognized the potential for contextual bias by document examiners. The contextual bias he recognized was induced by document examiners reading signatures rather than viewing them as pictorial forms. Dr. Fischhof's solution to this problem was to turn the comparison pages of signatures upside down so they were no longer legible writing. I have used this approach in several cases so that rather than subconsciously reading the writing, I am viewing the writing as tutorial elements. This approach is known as the Fischhof Method.

Framing the problem

The presentation of information is known as framing. When a problem is framed clearly and in a manner that appears to be logically sound, the problem solver will accept the framing and attempt to solve the problem in conjunction with the way the problem has been framed (Bernstein, 1996).

A Stanford University study tested the impact of framing a situation and then adding information about a decision to be made. Subjects were given enough information regarding a courtroom trial (Kahneman and Tversky, 1995). One group was given more detail regarding the defendant, and another group was given more information regarding the plaintiff.

Although the groups were told that the data was biased, they were unable to consider both sides and determine which one had better information. Both groups were influenced by the side having more information. (Kahneman and Tversky, 1995).

Webber (2008) reported, "Juries . . . typically base their decisions on whichever story seems most plausible to them, rather than weighing the evidence." They make their decisions regardless of whether the information is accurate.

McAuliff,et al. (2009) expanded on Webber's findings, stating that when jurors' motivation is low or their ability to understand the presented information is poor, they rely on heuristics and that which they understand as real-life situations (McAuliff et al., 2009). According to Black's Law Dictionary, heuristics is defined as, "the study of how people use their experience to answer questions and improve their performance." Merriam-Webster defines heuristic as, "involving or serving as an aid to learning, discovery, or problem-solving by experimental and especially trial-and-error methods." In other words, a heuristic is application of a rule-of-thumb to a topic. This may be knowledge learned from the television show, a movie, personal anecdotal data, or other non-evidentiary knowledge.

McAuliff et al., discovered that jurors are ". . . insensitive to the presence of a confound or experimenter bias in the expert's research." The jurors rely on their flawed analysis of the expert's evidence when rendering a verdict.

A sharp attorney can bias a jury by framing questions to the witness. Framing bias can cause the jury to view the expert as qualified or not qualified.

McAuliff et al. (2009) found a positive relationship between the juror's evaluation of experts' evidence and their verdicts. McAuliff reported that jurors are not able to evaluate statistical evidence and methodologies.

Further, he reported, "Judges are unable to differentiate between valid and junk science . . . leading to admission of invalid research at trial."

Document examiners who are most successful will understand these nuances and be able to reduce the potential biases of the triers of fact by presenting clear and easy to understand evidence to support their opinions.

Confirmation bias

Confirmation bias results when a person accepts evidence that supports their position and rejects evidence that does not support their position. Confirmation bias may appear when the document examiner presents only one side of the evidence in a report, commonly known as cherry picking.

As an example, if the retaining attorney told the document examiner, "My client said the signature on the contract is not his," the document examiner may present only exemplars that support the opinion that the attorney's client did not write the signature even though other exemplars refute the contention.

An example of confirmation bias occurred in one of my court cases requiring authentication of a will. The opposing document examiner had forty-three exemplars. He showed seven of the exemplars in his report. Citing those seven exemplars, he offered an opinion the decedent did not author the questioned signature (exclusion).

After we exchanged evidence, I used his other thirty-six exemplars to create exhibits that contradicted his opinion. The decedent had wide variability in his signatures.

The court ruled it was inconclusive whether the decedent had authored the signature.

In another case where I had more than one thousand exemplars, I opined the signature was not written by the person whose name was written on the page. In more than one thousand exemplars, significant attributes of the questioned signature were not present in the known signatures.

The opposing examiner received the same exemplars I received. He claimed that one signature out of all the exemplars confirmed the signature on the contract was authentic. To show this evidence, he literally turned the signature on the page so the attribute in the questioned signature seemed to match this one known signature. He manipulated the evidence.

I was able to show that his assertion was incorrect. He was exhibiting a confirmation bias by trying to sway the evidence to support the hypothesis of the attorney who had retained him.

The attorney who retained me won very large verdict plus punitive damages.

THE SCIENTIFIC METHOD

Many people don't know that science does not prove something is true. Science shows evidence that something is true.

Rigorous science always attempts to find evidence contradicting accepted fact or a hypothesis. Only when attempts to demonstrate contradictory evidence fails, does the scientist continue to accept the fact or hypothesis.

There is a key difference between working a document examination case and conducting a true scientific study. A scientific study is generally conducted double blind where neither the researcher nor the subject knows whether they are receiving real or counterfeit material. The double-blind approach reduces the effects of confirmation bias.

In document examination cases, blind examination studies are rare since the document examiner knows who is hiring them. An ideal situation would be for a third party to serve as an interface between the client, the attorney, and the document examiner. The document examiner would know neither the context of the case nor the requesting party.

Because most document examiners are sole proprietors, they tend to interface directly with the retaining party. As a result, they must be vigilant to avoid being swayed by the claims of the attorney's client.

In deposition, a document examiner stated, "I assume everyone is lying. The evidence is all that matters." This approach reduces the effects of confirmation bias.

When a scientific method is used in document examination cases, the methodology used in the examination is clearly stated in a report. The methodology can both be repeated by the document examiner and replicated by another document examiner. The purpose being to determine whether the same results are obtained when the steps are repeated or replicated. A scientific approach will list both supporting and non-supporting evidence. The results section will show why one side of the evidence is stronger than the other. This approach minimizes the document examiner's bias.

Chapter 15

Document examiner's reports

The result of the document examiner's investigation is a report of the findings and resultant opinion. If the document examiner has been designated in the case, the report is probably discoverable. Otherwise it may be considered attorney work product.

Clients do not always want a report if the findings fail to support the position set forth by the attorney's client's theory of the case.

Occasionally an attorney does not want a report in order to keep the details of the examiner's methodology from the opposing side. Instead, the examiner's testimony at deposition and trial, and the trial exhibits will serve as a report.

A report must demonstrate that the document examiner applied a scientific approach and applied generally accepted practices to the analysis. A full report provides detailed analysis of the work performed and the results. Demonstrative exhibits are included to support the methodology and opinions stated in the report.

An alternative to a report is a letter of opinion. A letter of opinion is a brief statement outlining the method used and opinion reached from the examination. The letter of opinion may list the questioned document(s) and known documents examined and a short analysis of the procedure followed and the results of the examination. It may be a one-page summary of the results. The letter of opinion may also be discoverable.

RULE 26 REPORT

A report must state the opinion in the form of an affidavit. Some jurisdictions require the report as an exhibit to the affidavit.

Federal court has clear requirements stated in Federal Rules of Civil Procedure Rule 26(a)(2)(B). Failure to follow the federal rules in federal court may cause denial of the report as evidence. State courts may have specific rules for expert reports.

It is important for the report to show that the examiner has taken a balanced approach to the case. As in scientific methodology, the methodology section should be clear enough so another examiner could reproduce the process to determine whether they come up with same or different results.

The results section of the report must show evidence that supports the opinion and evidence that refutes the opinion, followed by a discussion on why one outweighs the other and to what degree.

Too often expert reports only show evidence that supports the opinion. This presents the perception that the examiner has taken biased approach, whether that is true or not.

The expert's credibility on the witness stand can be impeached. The report must be free of any perception of confirmation bias in favor of the examiner's client.

Although these sections may not be mandatory in state court, it is helpful for the document examiner to use a format similar to:

1. Cover page. State the scope of the report and the opinion. This enables the reader to understand the summary and opinion without paging through the report.
2. Detailed scope of the examination. In-scope and out-of-scope statements may help clarify the boundaries of the research

examination. For example, "We want you to examine the signature for authenticity. We do not want you to examine the machine printed text." The signature is in scope. The machine printed text is out of scope.
3. Summary of the documents examined.
   a. One section to identify the questioned documents.
   b. One section to identify the known documents.
   c. For each document include:
      iv. The identification code assigned by the document examiner.
      v. Date of the document's creation or "date unknown."
      vi. Type or name of the document.
      vii. Original, photocopy, fax, NCR (no carbon required), etc.
      viii. Form of writing (print, cursive, manuscript, mixed).
4. Assumptions. For example, "An assumption is made that the documents presented as known signatures of (person's name) are true signatures of (person's name)." Unless the document examiner witnessed the person writing, the document examiner is taking someone's word that the signatures are authentic.
5. Limitations. For example, an indication of the type of documents used such as photocopies or the back pages of an NCR form.
6. Methodology used in the examination. This should be stated in enough detail for another document examiner to reproduce the methodology.
7. Results of the examination.
   a. Similarities.
   b. Differences.
8. Opinion. This must be stated using the nine options described in the SWGDOC standards or seven options in

the SAFE standards. If another standard, such as the FBI standard, is used, that standard must be referenced.
9. Affidavit.
10. Exhibits.
    a. Document examiner's CV.
    b. Questioned document(s).
    c. Known document(s).
    d. Supporting images showing how the opinion was reached.
    e. Any other exhibits to support the methodology and opinion.

Chapter 16

Selecting a document examiner

The document examiner you select can be a decisive factor whether you prevail in your case.

There is no licensing requirement for forensic document examiners. Professional trade organizations offer certifications. Some of these certifications are generally recognized in the industry as valid due to rigorous requirements prior to sitting for a comprehensive examination.

Others are given by unrecognized organizations or for-profit companies and are not considered valid indications of an examiner's level of proficiency.

When selecting a forensic document examiner as an expert witness or consultant, look for these key abilities. These will help improve your chances of prevailing with your case, provided your client's claim is meritorious.

Your chosen expert should have the ability to:

- Follow generally accepted practices
- Perform accurate assessments
- Ask the examiner to describe the methodology to be used for the case

FOLLOW A GENERALLY ACCEPTED PRACTICE

Your document examiner must follow a generally accepted practice for forensic document examiners.

In Frye v. U.S., 293 F.2d 1013 (D.C. CA 1923), the D.C. Court of Appeals adopted the test for "general acceptance." In California, the Kelly rule, People v. Kelly (1976) 17 Cal.3d 24, provides that expert testimony must be based on a technique that is "sufficiently established to have gained general acceptance in the particular field to which it belongs."

I testified where the opposing side's document examiner failed to follow generally accepted practice for handwriting identification of a questioned signature. The court ruled in a bench trial that the petitioner's document expert was more credible than the respondent's expert. The attorney who hired me prevailed in the case.

PERFORM ACCURATE ASSESSMENTS

A requirement of following generally accepted practice in forensics is for the examiner to perform accurate assessments of the data provided. As with any other profession, document examiners have a range of expertise and experience. As important as it is for your client to make a clear assessment of your abilities, it is up to you to determine in advance and with a high degree of accuracy whether the document examiner you plan to hire will perform the most accurate assessments and be ready to back up those assessments with a scientifically repeatable, reproducible and sound methodology in court.

ASK THE EXAMINER TO DESCRIBE THE METHODOLOGY TO BE USED FOR THE CASE

It is important for an attorney to ask an examiner to describe the methodology to be used researching the case. Ensure the methodology is generally accepted in the industry. The prospective document examiner should be able to cite authorities that support the claim the methodology is accepted in the practice of forensic document examination.

Establishing handwriting variability

An individual can only be eliminated as the writer of a questioned document once the range of variability of the known writer has been determined. Established authorities state that enough samples are required to show this variability. The number needed is case specific. I always ask for at least fifteen contemporaneous exemplars.

In the case mentioned above in which the opposing examiner did not follow generally accepted practices, the other document examiner eliminated the decedent as the writer of a holographic will. Her opinion was based on observed differences between two known signatures and the questioned signature.

Two samples are not sufficient to demonstrate a writer's range of variability. The examiner failed to state there were also differences between the two known signatures which were stipulated to have been written contemporaneously (in this case during the same sitting) by the decedent.

In accepted methodology, the basis of writer identification is to determine both similar and dissimilar traits in the questioned writing and the known writings. So, the variability in the author's known handwriting must also be analyzed.

Only then can it be determined with a degree of accuracy the extent to which the questioned writing has the same traits as and falls within the known variability of the known writing.

The opposing examiner in this case made no effort to determine the variability of the decedent's known handwriting. She made no attempt to examine the original will that was available in the court's records room.

I examined the original holographic will as required by the ASTM/SWGDOC standard E2290-07, *Standard Guide for Examination of Handwritten Items*, and displayed the scanned copy as an exhibit.

The other examiner failed to point out attributes of the questioned writing which also existed in the known writing. These attributes provided a strong probability that the will had been written by the decedent.

I presented exhibits showing 18 examples of the decedent's known handwriting. Many of these displayed attributes the other document examiner erroneously stated were not found in the questioned writing.

In this case, the other examiner used no generally accepted methodology.

Standard Guide for Examination of Handwritten Items, Standard E2290-07, item 7.5 states, "Determine whether the questioned writing is original writing. If it is not original writing, request the original." The standard states if the reproduction is not of "sufficient clarity for comparison purposes, discontinue these procedures."

The opposing examiner used a scanned image of a photo reduction of the original document. The original document showed characteristics that were not visible in this reproduction. Had the opposing examiner followed generally accepted practice by examining the known writing I examined, and the original will, she may have reached a different opinion than the one she stated.

A case of written initials

In another case in which I was retained as a rebuttal witness, the opposing document examiner eliminated the writer of initials on a document based upon three exemplars of the person's initials. He showed that there were differences between the known initials and the questioned initial. On rebuttal, I showed the court there were substantial differences among the three known initials. The exemplars were insufficient to determine the variability of the person's known writing.

As a result, there was no way to know whether the differences between the questioned initials and the known initials were merely another difference exhibited by the writer. I informed the court that based upon the insufficient number of exemplars and the observed differences among the known initials, the evidence only supported a possible opinion of inconclusive as to whether they questioned initials were written by the writer of the known initials.

The court ruled there was no evidence of forgery in this case. The reason given was the defendant's document examiner did not follow generally accepted practices. He did not examine a sufficient number of exemplars to determine the variability of the writer's initials.

CODE OF ETHICS

Members of National Association of Document Examiners, Scientific Association of Forensic Examiners, American Society of Questioned Document Examiners, and Association of Forensic Document Examiners subscribe to strict codes of ethics.

Make sure your document examiner is a member of an organization that requires adherence to a code of ethics.

On September 6, 2016, the United States Department of Justice and National Institute of Standards and Technology published an initial draft recommendation on National Code of Ethics and Professional Responsibility for the Forensic Sciences. This recommended code of ethics contains 16 points.

1. "Accurately represent his/her education, training, experience, and areas of expertise.
2. Pursue professional competency through training, proficiency testing, certification, and presentation and publication of research findings.
3. Commit to continuous learning in the forensic disciplines and stay abreast of new findings, equipment and techniques.
4. Promote validation and incorporation of new technologies, guarding against the use of non-valid methods in casework and the misapplication of validated methods.

5. Avoid tampering, adulteration, loss, or unnecessary consumption of evidentiary materials.
6. Avoid participation in any case where there are personal, financial, employment-related or other conflicts of interest.
7. Conduct full, fair and unbiased examinations, leading to independent, impartial, and objective opinions and conclusions.
8. Make and retain full, contemporaneous, clear and accurate written records of all examinations and tests conducted and conclusions drawn, in sufficient detail to allow meaningful review and assessment by an independent person competent in the field.
9. Base conclusions on generally-accepted procedures supported by sufficient data, standards and controls, not on political pressure or other outside influence.
10. Do not render conclusions that are outside one's expertise.
11. Prepare reports in unambiguous terms, clearly distinguishing data from interpretations and opinions, and disclosing all known associated limitations that prevent invalid inferences or mislead the judge or jury.
12. Do not alter reports or other records, or withhold information from reports for strategic or tactical litigation advantage.
13. Present accurate and complete data in reports, oral and written presentations and testimony based on good scientific practices and validated methods.
14. Communicate honestly and fully, once a report is issued, with all parties (investigators, prosecutors, defense attorneys, and other expert witnesses), unless prohibited by law.
15. Document and notify management or quality assurance personnel of adverse events, such as an unintended mistake or a breach of ethical, legal, scientific standards, or questionable conduct.

16. Ensure reporting, through proper management channels, to all impacted scientific and legal parties of any adverse event that affects a previously issued report or testimony."

CERTIFICATES AND EDUCATION

East Tennessee State University in Johnson City, TN offers a graduate school certificate in forensic document examination. The certificate is taught in the graduate school of criminal justice. Admission to the graduate school is required.

Document examiners have a variety of training and education. Although many have college degrees, these degrees are not necessarily in the sciences. A college degree is not generally required for certification. A college degree is required for document examiners according to the SWGDOC standard for training and education.

Some organizations, mostly those whose members are government and former government employed examiners, require a two-year apprenticeship under another document examiner. A difficulty with this requirement is that the training depends upon the skill, knowledge, and teaching ability of the trainer. There is also no uniform method of training across government agencies. As an example, the FBI, Postal Service, and Secret Service all have their own training manuals. Local law enforcement and forensics laboratories have their own training manuals. In some instances, such as the United States Army, only fifteen weeks of internship is included in this two years of training. Forty-two weeks of self-study is included in the two-years of training.

The standard states that the equivalent of two years of training may be substituted for the training. There is no definition of the meaning of equivalent.

In November 2017 I was subjected to a Dauber challenge to my qualifications to testify as an expert in a case involving a signature on a contract. The basis of the challenge was that I do not have the stated two years of formal training as defined in the SWGDOC standard. The judge in the federal district court ruled, "Mr. Wakshull has been a forensic document examiner since 2010, has attended numerous seminars and conferences on forensic document examination, has testified as an expert many times, and completed a graduate certificate in forensic document examination. Mr. Wakshull's training, although not a formal apprenticeship, is likely the equivalent of such given his involvement in the field for the past seven years. Based on his experience, the Court finds his testimony admissible under Rule 702."

Some forensic document examination organizations offer certification to members. Certification demonstrates achievement of a level of expertise proven by passing a comprehensive examination. Some organizations, such as National Association of Document Examiners, require passing an examination plus a mock trial or deposition testimony to achieve certification.

Legitimate certifications are recognized in the industry. They are offered by non-profit trade organizations who do not generate profit resulting from members' certification. These organizations post a list of members with earned certification on their websites.

Check the organization's website to learn whether they offer certification for forensic document examination. There are document examiners who claim to have certification and diplomate status from an organization that does not even mention forensic document examination on the website.

Certified document examiners must maintain continuing education in their discipline to maintain certification.

Beware of examiners who claim they are certified by for profit schools. Learn whether these schools require students to obtain continuing education to maintain their certification. Often the certification is merely a certificate of completion of the school's classes.

Not all forensic examiners supply CVs containing honest, accurate information. In one of my cases, the opposing examiner stated she had worked cases in several states. In deposition, this

Californiabased document examiner was asked to describe the Pennsylvania case she had worked on. Although her CV listed such a case, her response was, "I have no idea what you are talking about."

Other document examiners state they have worked on a large number of cases. One document examiner claims he worked on more than fourteen thousand cases in forty-one years. This equals more than three hundred fifty cases per year each year for forty years. How can a person work on a case each day of the year and find time to testify in court and at deposition?

Another document examiner claimed that when she worked for a government agency, she worked one hundred cases per month. That is approximately five cases per day.

Always divide the number of cases by the number of years they have been in practice to discover whether the stated number is realistic. How many cases per day would be required to complete the total number of stated cases? You will often find a discrepancy in this information.

INVESTIGATE YOUR PROSPECTIVE DOCUMENT EXAMINER

The Internet is a valuable resource for finding a qualified document examiner for your case. Search engines such as Google, Yahoo, Bing, etc. make it easy to find document examiners. As an attorney, you have access to LEXIS-NEXIS. Use this service to find cases on which document examiner worked.

It is incumbent on the attorney or other prospective employer of the document examiner to ensure the document examiner has the required background and is free of potential liabilities which may arise in deposition or trial.

INTERNET SEARCH METHODOLOGY

Begin your investigation once you receive the prospective document examiner's CV.

Type the document examiner's name and company name into the search engine. The attorney on the other side of the case should also be performing this task. Proper due diligence can save you embarrassing revelations brought forth by the opposing counsel.

I always advise my clients of this and it has often paid off by providing evidence that can be used in court to discredit and sometimes disqualify the opposing expert. In a recent case, the opposing examiner claimed to have certification from a forensics organization. During cross-examination, he was presented with an article showing a PBS Frontline investigation of the organization. The reporter's house cat had received a certification in forensics from that organization.

Although the document examiner was not disqualified from testifying, his credibility was severely damaged.

As you search, know that a premier location on the search page does not necessarily mean the person is qualified to perform the work. Some document examiners purchase enough advertising through search engines to achieve superior placement. Their listings are identified as advertisements.

Below these paid ads are results of the organic searches, which might be paid. Superior organic search results can be achieved by successful adherence to the unpublished search engine algorithms. Companies often hire experts to help them achieve prominent positions in the organic search results.

Always apply the same due diligence to investigate the expert's qualifications whether you found them in the paid listings or the organic listings.

To ensure a thorough search, enter these items into several Internet search engines since the engines provide different information.

1. The person's name using various spellings. For example, if the person's first name is Mike, also search for Michael.
2. The name of the school where the person received education and training.

In deposition and in court I have been asked about the curriculum from East Tennessee State University where I received part of my education and training. The curriculum is available on the school's website. The opposing attorney wants to show whether my response matches the facts.

Always determine whether the expert's school offers a full curriculum as recommended by ASTM/SWGDOC standard.

Your due diligence must go further to validate the information in the examiner's CV. Still using the Internet, examine the organizations to which the document examiner belongs to determine whether the organization is legitimate.

For example, the American College of Forensic Examiners Institute (ACFEI) offers several certifications. None of these certifications are for questioned documents. Note: Do not confuse AFCEI with AFCE. AFCE is the Association of Certified Fraud Examiners.

There are document examiners who state they are certified and hold a diplomate certificate from ACFEI. This means only that they demonstrated the following. They:

- Worked for three years in a "forensic related field."
- Passed a certification exam with nothing to do with document examination.
- Provided a properly funded check to the organization for $250.

Organizations such as National Association of Document Examiners, Scientific Association of Forensic Examiners, American Board of Forensic Document Examiners, and Board of Forensic Document Examiners offer legitimate industry certifications for forensic document examination.

Be wary of document examiners who claim certification from other organizations.

A document examiner in Southern California places "Dr." in front of her name and "PhDC" after her name. However, one of her online CVs lists a bachelor's degree. Another lists a doctorate from a non-existent university.

A Google search of a document examiner in Texas found a case in which the appellate court in United States of America v. Mary Revels found the document examiner unqualified to testify. When the retaining counsel requested a continuance to retain a different document examiner, the Court refused the continuance. The Court wrote:

> "Although the Court appreciates Defendant's recent efforts to obtain a substitute document examiner, the Court concludes her request for a second continuance should be denied. ... Minimal research into [document examiner's] qualifications and credibility would have unearthed the concerns brought to the forefront by the Government at Defendant's sentencing hearing. The predicament Defendant has now found herself in and the resulting delay could have been avoided had she been more thorough in investigating the background of her initial opinion witness, and, having done so and identified the potential red flags, considered a suitable alternative in the event the Court determined the witness was not qualified." [I removed the examiner's name]

Had the defense counsel performed proper due diligence on their document examiner, they could have prevented the problems at the hearing.

The required research is simple and straightforward and should always be performed prior to selecting any forensic expert.

If you discover negative comments about a document examiner on websites where any person can post feedback, ask the document examiner about the feedback. The comments may not be legitimate. As an example, several years ago I discovered a negative comment about my company. The name used by the person, an alleged client, who posted the comment was unknown to me. I contacted the owner of the website and explained that I did not recognize the name. The website's owner removed the comment.

IS YOUR FIRST QUESTION THE CORRECT QUESTION?

When searching for a qualified document examiner, often the first question an attorney asks is, "How much does it cost to examine a signature (or other subject of the examination)?"

This is the wrong question. It is similar to a prospective client asking an attorney to quote the complexity of a case before the attorney has seen the details.

Most document examiners charge an hourly rate, as do most attorneys. Unless a flat fee is charged, an honest document examiner cannot answer this question without seeing the case since the time involved depends on the complexity of the case.

Most document examiners charge a minimum nonrefundable retainer fee. Ask the document examiner to forward a retainer agreement and fee schedule. A good fee schedule will have a simple calculation method rather than a complex structure of different fees for different work. Often, there is a rate for research and travel and a second rate for testimony.

Some document examiners will quote a flat fee for the examination. When a flat fee is advertised, request the complete fee schedule. Some examiners charge a low examination fee to win the bid and charge high fees for "additional work." They may also charge a separate high fee for designation and testimony.

Be aware of bait and switch. Always make sure you are comparing apples to apples when evaluating prospective document examiners. If you select an expert based on a flat fee of $500, you are likely to discover this will not represent the total cost of the work required work.

If a prospective attorney client brought a case to your firm and subsequently chose to go with a competing attorney who quoted a total fee of $500 for work of an unknown scope, what would be your advice?

SERVICES AND DELIVERABLES YOU SHOULD EXPECT FROM YOUR DOCUMENT EXAMINER

- *Continuous communication*: The document examiner must communicate with you, the client, about all aspects of the case. The document examiner becomes an integral part of the theme of your case. He or she must understand your theme and be able to communicate how their research integrates and supports it. You, as the client, must also communicate with the document examiner. This includes proper preparation prior to all testimony. Preparation of all parties must be done ahead of testimony rather than the day of testimony. Early preparation provides the attorney and the witness time to resolve any potential difficulties, and time to reflect on the preparation.
- *Timely attention to your case*: The document examiner must meet all required milestones for case deliverables. Make sure the document examiner can dedicate the required time to your case.
- *Instructions for obtaining necessary documents for research*: The document examiner will provide instructions for obtaining exemplars for the case. This ensures the case is sound and not subject to a challenge due to improper exemplars.
- *A comprehensive report (if a report is required)*: The report must be complete, describing all methods used, reasons for the opinion reached and list all supporting exhibits. The report must comply with all applicable rules of court for the jurisdiction.
- *Questions to ask the opposing examiner*: The document examiner will review the report from the opposing examiner and

generate questions to ask the opposing examiner in deposition and cross examination.

- *Questions to ask your document examiner on direct examination*: Your document examiner will prepare a list of questions to ask on direct examination. These questions include areas of potential weakness in the examiner's background or the examination methodology. Asking these questions on direct examination allows the examiner to answer the questions in a friendly environment rather than on cross examination.

Questions to ask your prospective document examiner

- *Ask the prospective document examiner how he or she qualifies according to these requirements.* How do you comply with Federal Rules of Evidence 702, California Evidence Code 720(a), other jurisdictional rules, or ASTM Standard E444. These documents state that an expert must be able to demonstrate skill, special knowledge, education, experience or training in the field in which the expert testifies. Note the conjunction or between the requirements. Only one is required, yet more than one is better and all five is best.
- *Describe your training and education in document examination and related subjects.* ASTM/SWGDOC Standard E2388 outlines the minimum training and education requirements for forensic document examiners. If the document examiner does not have the two years training, ask how they satisfy the equivalent of two years training. Has any court ruled that satisfied the equivalent of the two years training? Ask for evidence of the ruling. The National Academy of Sciences stated training is secondary to education for the forensic sciences.
- *Is the document examiner trained in research methods and science?* Document examiners are researchers and investigators.

They must apply a science-based approach to the case. Ask the prospective document examiner to describe the scientific method they use when examining documents.

- *Describe your methodology.* Learn how the document examiner conducts research. Is the methodology based on a generally accepted practice in the industry? Is the methodology reproducible by another document examiner in a manner enabling that another examiner can to reach the same conclusion opinion when they follow the methodology? Is there a standard operating procedure for the methodology?
- *What tools does the document examiner use?* In one case, the opposing document examiner admitted in deposition that he did not own the tools necessary to conduct the examination.
- *Can the document examiner demonstrate specialized knowledge of the discipline?* Can the document examiner cite authorities to support the opinion, or is the opinion simply based on the document examiner's belief? Does the document examiner know the source of the information that supports the opinion?
- *Does the document examiner publish in peer reviewed journals or present at conferences before peers?*
- *Does the document examiner perform research in the field of forensic document examination?* Is the research presented to peers for review?
- *What education supports the document examiner's ability to perform forensic document examination?* Education may be in document examination and related subjects. Some related subjects are chemistry for performing ink analysis, physics to understand analysis using different light frequencies, physiology to understand the motor coordination of writing, computer imaging for analyzing digital images, and many others. Education must always include comprehensive education in forensic document examination. Ask the document examiner how he or she remains current in the field.

- *What format will be used for your document examiner's report?* A report must be clear and succinct. Long, voluminous reports are difficult to read and understand. The report must be written in language understandable to the layperson rather than the reader of a professional journal.
- *What types of demonstrative exhibits are created?* Demonstrative exhibits show the trier of fact how the opinion was reached. Properly prepared exhibits can educate the trier of fact to the development and underlying basis of an expert's opinion.
- *Is the document examiner certified?* Ask the document examiner whether he or she is certified by a document examination organization. Private examiners are certified by organizations such as National Association of Document Examiners and Scientific Association of Forensic Examiners, whereas examiners with government experience may be certified by the American Board of Forensic Document Examiners. Other document examiners may hold a university level certificate in forensic document examination. Any of these demonstrates a high level of specialized training. Be wary of individuals who hold a certification from a "diploma mill" or for-profit companies. These "certifications" may simply be certificates of completion for a class.
- *Does the document examiner stay current in the discipline?* Conferences and university classes are excellent ways for the document examiner to maintain currency in the field. Many conferences offer full-day hands-on workshops in conjunction with the conference. Bar association seminars are an excellent means of staying current with legal trends and requirements for the expert's attorney clients.
- *Request a copy of the document examiner's current CV.*
- *Ask the document examiner for a sample report used in trial and is public record.*

Chapter 17

Final thoughts

Forensic document examination is a technical discipline requiring the examiner to have high skill. Variability of writing cannot be determined by a simple visual examination. The experience, knowledge and skill of a trained document examiner is needed to identify and articulate the intricacies that define a common or not common author.

Tools and techniques used by skilled document examiners today are different and more precise than those used by document examiners in the past. Advances in computer hardware and software provide means of more precisely comparing handwriting than previously used methods which were difficult and cumbersome.

Powerful digital microscopes combined with software such as Adobe Photoshop permit document examiners to quickly learn the intricacies of a document. Software development such as NEGA from Spain provide document examiners the ability to learn aspects of writing that were otherwise difficult to know.

When hiring a document examiner as a consultant or designated expert witness, make sure the document examiner maintains competency in these tools and techniques. In trial the opposing document examiner stated in testimony that my approach was not generally accepted in the industry. He stated that his approach had been used for the last 50 years. In my testimony I agreed that 50 years ago they did use the approach he was using. He did not stay current in techniques used by modern document examiners. The jury ruled in favor of the attorney who retained me.

Although the courts require expert witnesses to use a scientific approach, performing an examination of documents is rarely done in this manner. A pure scientific approach requires a double-blind experiment in which neither the person hiring the document examiner nor the document examiner are given information about the case.

A scientific approach is possible and desirable. It can be applied to a case by establishing a hypothesis and then setting out to refute it. Each case is treated as a unique research project, the result of which is an opinion based strictly on the evidence provided to the document examiner. Ask your prospective examiner to describe how a scientific approach will be applied to your case. Make sure the document examiner's loyalty is to the evidence in not your client's desired outcome. Biases will likely be exposed in deposition and/or trial.

Examination of handwriting may involve subjectivity. The National Academy of Sciences reported that many forensic sciences, including handwriting examination, often are performed using an approach that is too subjective. Use of a repeatable and reproducible methodology reduces the subjectivity of the examination.

The document examiner can use quantitative methods when needed, to improve the accuracy of the opinion. Quantitative methods include calculating proportional relationships among the zones of handwriting and measuring slant angles of characters. Use of software to overlay known and questioned writing enables the document examiner to provide the client with exhibits which demonstrate the reason for their opinion.

The document examiner must know of potential bias induced by knowing the client's desired results. The examiner is an advocate for the evidence itself, rather than the hiring attorney or the attorney's client. The focus of the work is to determine whether the evidence supports the client's position.

Document examination involves more than examination of handwriting. Work is often performed to determine the type of printer used, whether a document has been altered, whether the document was constructed using computer techniques or if it is truly the document purported.

The document examiner you hire must have enough skill to examine more than the expected scope of work. Examination of handwriting may require analyzing the associated machine printing on the page or determining whether the signature on the page is ink or was produced by a print process. Determining the order in which overlapping signatures or other written lines were placed onto the page may need to be performed.

Document examination is an investigative science. The required knowledge is rapidly changing due to the proliferation of technology, computer generated documents, and electronic signature pads. It takes skill, knowledge, and experience for a document examiner to provide the highest degree of service to a client. Document examiners must attend sufficient training and education classes to maintain proficiency in the discipline.

A document examiner must be able to communicate clearly with people not educated in the technical terminology of the field. Make sure the document examiner you hire can teach the triers of fact and the attorneys managing the case using common language and clear, demonstrative exhibits.

For questions about material in this book, contact Mike Wakshull at mikew@quality9.com or visit https://quality9.com to send a question. Your feedback is welcome.

References

Ariely, D. 2008. Predictably Irrational: The Hidden Forces That Shape Our Decisions. New York, N.Y: Harper Perennial.
Arzy, S., Brezis, M., Khoury, S., Simon, S. & Ben-Hur, T. 2009. "Misleading One Detail: A Preventable Mode of Diagnostic Error?". Journal of Evaluation in Clinical Practice 15: 804–809.
Baer, M. A. 2005. "Is An Independent Medical Examination Independent?" The Forensic Examiner Winter: 33.
Cialdini, R. 2001. Influence: Science and Practice. Boston: Allyn & Bacon.
Crisp. 2003. United States v. Crisp. 324 F.3d 261
Denbeaux, M. P., Risinger, M. D. 2003. "Kumho Tire And Expert Reliability: How the Question You Ask Gives the Answer You Get." Seaton Hall Law Review 34(1): 15–75.
Dyer, A. G., Found, B & Rogers, D. 2006. "Visual Attention and Expertise for Forensic Signature Analysis." Journal of Forensic Sciences 51(6): 1397–1404.
Eliot, T. S. 1943. Little Gidding in Four Quartets. Harcourt: San Diego.
Found, B. & Bird, C. 2016. The Modular Forensic Handwriting Method. Journal of Forensic Document Examination, 26: 7–83.
Found, B. & Rogers, D. 2008. "The Probative Character of Forensic Handwriting Examiners' Identification And Elimination Options On Questioned Signatures." Forensic Science International 178: 54–60.
Freeman, F. N. 1914. The Teaching of Handwriting. Boston. Houghton Mifflin Company.

Garner, B. A. (editor) 2009. Black's Law Dictionary Ninth Edition. St. Paul: Thompson Reuters.

Giannelli, Paul C. 2008. "Confirmation Bias in Forensic Testing." GP Solo 25(2): 22–23.

Harrison, W. 1981. Suspect Documents, Their Scientific Examination. Chicago: Nelson-Hall Publishers.

Hilton, O. 1995. "The Relationship of Mathematical Probability to The Handwriting Identification Problem." International Journal of Forensic Document Examiners. (1 July/Sept) 3: 224–229.

Hilton, O. 1993. Scientific Examination of Documents. Revised Edition. Boca Raton: CRC Press.

Huber, R. A. & Headrick, A. M. 1999. Handwriting Identification: Facts and Fundamentals. New York: CRC Press.

Jindal, D. Kuar, H & Chattopadhyay, P.K. 1999. "A Metric Analysis of Handwriting: A Study of Signatures." International Journal of Forensic Document Examiners 5:105–107.

Kahneman, D., & Tversky, A. 1995. "Conflict Resolution: A Cognitive Perspective." In Barriers to Conflict Resolution, edited by Arrow, K. Mnookin, R, Ross, L., Tversky, A, Wilson, R, 44–60. New York, NY: W. W. Norton & Company, Inc.

Kam, M. Weinstein, J. & Conn, R. 1994. "Proficiency Of Professional Document Examiners In Writer Identification." Journal of Forensic Sciences 39(1): 5–14.

McAlexander, T.V. 1999. "Explaining Qualified Handwriting Opinions To The Jury." International Journal of Forensic Document Examiners 5: 20–21.

McAuliff, B. D., Kovera, M. B. & Nunez, G. 2009. "Can Jurors Recognize Missing Control Groups, And Experimenter Bias In Psychological Science." Law and Human Behavior 33: 247–257.

National Research Council. 2009. Strengthening Forensic Science In The United States: A Path Forward. Washington, D.C. The National Academy Press.

National Commission on Forensic Science. 2016. Testimony Using the Term Reasonable Scientific Certainty. https://www.justice.gov/ncfs/file/816021/download.

Osborn, A. S. 1929. Questioned Documents. 2nd ed. Albany, NY: Boyd Printing Company.

Project Management Institute. 2013. A Guide to the Project Management Body of Knowledge. 5th ed. Newtown Square: Project Management Institute.

Raines, K. 2006. Forgery: Crime Solving Science Experiments. Berkeley Heights, New Jersey: Enslow Publishers.

Risinger, M. J., Denbeaux, M. P. & Saks, M. D. 1989. "Exorcism of Ignorance as a Proxy for Rational Knowledge: The Lessons of Handwriting Identification Expertise". University of Pennsylvania Law Review 137: 731–787.

Risinger, M. J. & Saks, M. D. 1996. "Science and Nonscience in The Courts: Daubert Meets Handwriting Identification Expertise." Iowa Law Review. 82(21): 1–52.

Srihari, S. N; Cha, S, Arora, H. & Lee, S. 2002. "Individuality In Handwriting." Journal of Forensic Sciences 47(4): 1–17.

Schwab, A. P., 2008. "Putting Cognitive Psychology To Work: Improving Decision-Making In The Medical Encounter." Social Science & Medicine 67: 1861-1869

Starzecpyzel, 1995. United States v. Starzecpyzel, 880 F. Supp. 1027 (S.D.N.Y. 1995).

Webber, S. 2008. "The Dark Side Of Optimism; Why Looking On The Bright Side Keeps Us From Thinking Critically." The Conference Board Review 45: 30-36.

Index

A

altered document 151
American College of Forensic Examiners Institute (ACFEI) 181
American Society of Questioned Document Examiners (ASQDE) 8, 175
Analysis, Comparison, Examination, and Verification (ACE-V) 137
analysis of handwriting 1, 14
angle of writing 75
ASTM 16, 30, 48, 51, 53, 65, 77, 132, 133, 136, 142, 146, 159, 173, 181, 185
attorney 6, 7, 8, 11, 21, 47, 48, 57, 62, 63, 84, 87, 153, 157, 159, 161, 162, 164, 165, 167, 172, 179, 181, 183, 184, 187, 190, 191
authenticate 1, 18, 21, 57
　definition 21
authentication 21, 22, 25, 78
　definition in California Code 25

Index

authenticity 1, 2, 13, 14, 18, 21, 36, 37, 51, 58, 86, 124, 133, 152, 160, 161, 169
  of signatures 14

B

baseline 65
bias 1, 18, 20, 47, 72, 135, 143, 148, 156, 157, 158, 159, 161, 162, 164, 165, 166, 168, 191, 193
  actual bias 157
  advocate's bias 157
  anchoring 161
  cognitive bias 157, 160, 162
  confirmation bias 148, 164
  contextual bias 161
  Fischhof Method 163
  framing bias 164
  implied bias 158
  inferential bias 158
  judicial bias 158
  juries 163
  laboratory bias 159
  presumed bias 158
Black's Law Dictionary 12, 14, 16, 21, 25, 156, 157, 158, 164, 193
blobs 71
brain writing 50
Brugnatelli 73

C

calipers 45
celebrities 57

Index

check 22, 54, 56, 62, 65, 98, 162, 181
class characteristic 65, 89
code of ethics 8, 9, 175
common features 136, 160
computer 1, 4, 17, 26, 39, 40, 42, 43, 49, 69, 96, 97, 101, 102, 119, 120, 124, 128, 134, 186, 189, 191, 206
conclusive evidence 74
contract 11, 22, 24, 54, 63, 80, 83, 94, 98, 101, 118, 153, 162, 165, 177
Crisp 144, 192
cut and paste 95, 97, 99, 100, 101

D

Daubert 1, 27, 28, 138, 139, 144, 146, 147, 148, 150, 194
dictation 54
digital forensic imaging 22
digital tablet 17, 57, 119, 120, 121, 123
disguised writing 63, 83, 143
document 1, 2, 4, 6, 7, 11, 12, 13, 16, 17, 18, 25, 29, 30, 31, 46, 49, 51, 53, 58, 77, 81, 115, 119, 138, 139, 144, 146, 150, 152, 154, 171, 172, 173, 177, 178, 179, 181, 183, 185, 186, 187, 206, 207
  definition 16
document examiners' opinions 20, 34. *See also* **qualified opinions**
duplicate 23, 24, 26, 27, 60, 63, 100
  definition in Federal Rules 23
  definition in Louisiana Code 27

E

education requirements 185

Index

electromagnetic spectrum 92, 93, 104
Electrostatic Detection Device (ESDA) 43
eliminate 14, 21, 22, 34, 36, 37, 138
elimination 36, 37, 192
email 13, 24, 127, 129
  authentication of 128
error rate 28, 147, 148, 150, 151, 152, 153, 155
errors 150, 151, 152, 154, 162
  grammatical 162
  typographical 162
exemplar 7, 11, 18, 36, 37, 38, 47, 48, 50, 51, 52, 53, 54, 55, 56, 57, 58, 60, 62, 63, 65, 84, 85, 86, 98, 117, 123, 133, 136, 151, 152, 160, 165, 173, 174, 184
  definition 51
  number of 7, 36, 37, 151, 175
expert 1, 2, 3, 4, 6, 10, 14, 22, 25, 27, 29, 78, 131, 138, 144, 145, 146, 147, 148, 150, 156, 157, 158, 160, 161, 164, 168, 171, 172, 176, 177, 180, 182, 183, 185, 187, 189, 190
expertise and experience 172
expert witness 1, 4, 6, 10, 25, 138, 150, 158, 171, 176, 189, 190

F

false negative 151
false positive 151
fatigue 71
Federal Rules of Evidence 17, 23, 25, 27, 145, 147, 185
Fischhof Method 163
  bias reduction 162
forensic 2, 4, 6, 7, 9, 12, 13, 16, 17, 18, 21, 25, 28, 30, 31, 46, 49, 51, 53, 58, 77, 81, 115, 119, 138, 139, 143, 146, 150, 152, 154, 160, 171, 172, 173, 177, 178, 181, 185, 186, 187, 190, 206, 207

Index

forensic document examination 2, 4, 13, 16, 49, 53, 119, 139, 154, 173, 177, 178, 181, 186, 187, 206, 207
forge 79
forgery 2, 79, 83, 175
  auto 83
Found and Rogers 143, 144
Frye 1, 27, 29, 138, 146, 147, 172

G

generally accepted practice 31, 172, 174, 186
genuineness of a writing 25
  definition in California Code 25
gloves 45
goop 68, 69
graphic maturity 70

H

handwriting 1, 2, 3, 4, 7, 8, 11, 13, 14, 18, 24, 25, 26, 33, 36, 48, 49, 50, 51, 53, 54, 55, 56, 58, 63, 64, 67, 68, 70, 71, 76, 78, 85, 97, 111, 121, 138, 139, 140, 141, 142, 143, 144, 172, 173, 189, 190, 191
Hilton 48, 69, 77, 140, 193
Hitler diaries 8
holographic will 11, 37, 94, 173
Howard Hughes
  autobiography 8
  diary 8
HSI Examiner 44, 93
Huber and Hedrick 52, 74, 76, 77, 141, 149
Hyperspectral imaging system 44
hypothesis 19, 20, 142, 143, 148, 165, 190

Index

I

identification 8, 20, 24, 48, 49, 50, 53, 58, 67, 70, 73, 76, 77, 78, 89, 111, 115, 134, 140, 141, 143, 169, 172, 173
identify 14, 21, 22, 34, 37, 49, 70, 88, 93, 99, 115, 138, 139, 141, 142, 169, 189
illness 71, 85
individual characteristic 89
infirmity 85
informal writing 54
infrared 39, 40, 43, 44, 92, 93, 94, 104
  infrared light 44, 92, 93, 94, 105
initials 53, 63, 90, 174
ink 13, 16, 18, 42, 56, 68, 93, 94, 97, 103, 106, 108, 109, 111, 113, 114, 115, 116, 119, 121, 123, 152, 186, 191
ink jet printer 17
Institute of Electrical and Electronic Engineers (IEEE) 49
International Graphonomics Society 49
Internet 6, 129, 179, 180

J

JonBenét Ramsey 8
JPEG 123, 124, 129, 134
JPG 134
junk science 28, 164

K

Kam 139, 142, 193
known documents 50, 51, 85, 90, 133, 155, 168, 169
known writing 14, 18, 21, 34, 37, 42, 47, 48, 51, 57, 67, 69, 70, 71, 72, 73, 74, 75, 80, 81, 84, 87, 135, 151, 173, 174
Kumho Tire versus Carmichael 29, 150

Index

L

laser printer 102
legal document 54
letter of opinion 167, 168
Lindberg baby kidnapping 8
line sequence 83, 102, 106, 108
Louisiana Code of Evidence 26
Loupe 41

M

mathematics 48, 49, 77, 140
measurements 41, 75, 140, 141
medication 86
memorabilia 57
Michael Risinger 138
Michael Saks 138
microscope 15, 39, 41, 42, 44, 47, 63, 66, 69, 84, 102, 103, 107, 113, 115, 116, 117
Mormon Will 8

N

National Academy of Sciences (NAS) 1, 143, 160, 185, 190
National Association of Document Examiners (NADE) 8, 54, 175, 178, 181, 187, 206
National Institute of Justice (NIJ) 21
National Institute of Standards and Technology (NIST) 9, 16, 31, 41, 175
  Standard ruler 41
natural variation 34, 71, 74, 139, 140
NEGA software 83, 108, 189
ninhydrin 152

Index

no carbon required (NCR) 98, 169

O

Organization of Scientific Area Committees (OSAC) 31
original 23, 24, 26, 27, 45, 48, 62, 96, 97, 99, 101, 111, 115, 116, 119, 158, 173, 174
  definition in Federal Rules 23
  definition in Louisiana Code 26
  definition in Texas Code 26
Osborn 72, 77, 140, 141, 193

P

paper dating 112
PDF 17, 24, 56, 123, 124, 125, 129, 134
photocopier 113
photocopy 1, 17, 37, 45, 56, 91, 97, 98, 99, 100, 109, 112, 114, 115, 116, 159, 169
Photoshop 22, 42, 56, 69, 79, 82, 87, 90, 96, 97, 98, 101, 109, 111, 116, 124, 125, 130, 134, 135, 136, 189
pixel 96, 117, 134
pixels per inch 117, 134
probability theory 48
proficiency test 149, 154

Q

qualified 6, 20, 22, 36, 63, 123, 144, 179, 183
qualified opinion 20, 22, 36, 63, 123
questioned document 21, 38, 50, 60, 62, 64, 76, 81, 90, 115, 135, 136, 139, 152, 155, 158, 162, 167, 173
questioned writing 14, 18, 34, 37, 42, 47, 48, 51, 52, 55, 58, 59, 60, 62, 67, 69, 70, 71, 72, 73, 74, 76, 80, 81, 85, 87, 135,

138, 149, 151, 173, 190

R

report 5, 10, 17, 18, 20, 22, 46, 52, 55, 59, 127, 142, 143, 148, 151, 152, 153, 160, 164, 166, 167, 168, 176, 184, 187
request exemplars 54, 59, 60, 62, 63
Risinger and Saks 138, 139, 140, 142, 143
robosigning 89
rubber stamp 90, 118
Rule 26 Report 168

S

sampling 120
Sargon Enterprises 146
scanner 42, 43, 129, 134
scientific approach 1, 18, 76, 123, 140, 143, 162, 166, 167, 190
Scientific Association of Forensic Examiners (SAFE) 8, 16, 24, 31, 32, 34, 58, 81, 132, 133, 136, 142, 170, 175, 181, 187, 206
scientific method 72, 138, 143, 148, 166, 186
Scientific Working Group for Forensic Document Examination (SWGDOC) 13, 16, 24, 30, 31, 32, 33, 34, 48, 58, 65, 77, 81, 132, 133, 136, 142, 145, 169, 173, 177, 181, 185
security markers 115, 118
signature 13, 14, 17, 22, 37, 38, 46, 47, 48, 51, 52, 53, 54, 55, 57, 60, 62, 63, 65, 69, 72, 73, 74, 75, 79, 80, 82, 83, 84, 85, 86, 88, 89, 97, 98, 100, 101, 103, 106, 108, 116, 119, 120, 121, 123, 133, 135, 140, 144, 152, 160, 165, 169, 172, 173, 177, 183, 191
  definition 14
  stylized 84
simulate 59, 82

Index

simulation 72, 79, 82, 83
   auto 83
special cause variation 86
Srihari 49, 141, 194
standard operating procedure (SOP) 132, 133, 136, 137, 148, 186
Starzecpyzel 28, 29, 139, 146, 149, 194
strong probability 34, 37, 81, 174
stylus 120

T

TIFF 124, 129, 134
trash marks 113, 114
tremor 85, 86

U

ultraviolet 39, 40, 43, 93
unqualified 21, 22, 34, 36, 182
unqualified opinion 21, 22, 36

V

variability 7, 36, 48, 66, 67, 69, 71, 72, 73, 74, 75, 81, 86, 136, 140, 151, 165, 173, 174
   common cause 72, 86
   inter-writer 140, 141
   intra-writer 67, 71, 73, 74, 76, 136, 140, 141
   special cause 71
video spectral comparator (VSC) 43, 44, 93, 106
visible light 44, 92, 93

Index

W

watermarks 112
wax printer 102
writing 14, 17, 18, 21, 36, 37, 42, 43, 47, 48, 52, 55, 57, 58, 59, 60, 62, 67, 69, 70, 71, 72, 73, 75, 76, 80, 81, 84, 85, 87, 135, 138, 149, 151, 173, 174, 190
  definition in California Code 17, 25
  definition in Federal Rules 23
  definition in Louisiana Code 26
  definition in Texas Code 26

Z

Zodiac Killer 57
zones 65, 77, 190
  lower zone 65, 66, 70
  middle zone 65, 74
  upper zone 65, 74

About the Author

Mike Wakshull is a practicing civil and criminal court-qualified forensic document examiner based in Temecula, California. He partners with legal clients to dissect evidence in handwritten and computer-generated questioned documents.

His background includes founding a computer graphics software company and a project management consulting and training business. His work as a corporate trainer in information systems and project management took him to four continents. He managed global information systems policies and corporate quality risk management for a large biotechnology company. He applies skills from quality engineering, scientific training and information systems to forensic document examination.

He is vice president of the Scientific Association of Forensic Examiners, and international forensic document examination association with members in 10 countries. He frequently speaks before his peers and legal professionals at conferences and seminars.

Wakshull served as chair of the 2012 National Association of Document Examiners conference and is past president of the San

Diego Chapter of Forensic Expert Witness Association. He has been an invited speaker at many national and international conferences. Wakshull was the only document examiner from the United States to speak at the World Congress of Forensics in China in October 2011.

He holds a Master of Science degree in technology management from the University of Denver, a graduate school certificate in forensic document examination from East Tennessee State University and is a certified quality engineer.

Wakshull is on the adjunct faculty of the University of Redlands and is a member of the National Speakers Association.

www.ingramcontent.com/pod-product-compliance
Lightning Source LLC
Chambersburg PA
CBHW040321300426
44112CB00020B/2828